STUPID CELEBRITIES

OTHER BOOKS BY KATHRYN AND ROSS PETRAS

The 776 Stupidest Things Ever Said
The 776 Even Stupider Things Ever Said
The 776 Nastiest Things Ever Said
The 176 Stupidest Things Ever Done
Very Bad Poetry
Stupid Sex

STUPID CELEBRITIES

Over 500 of the Most Idiotic Things
Ever Said by Famous People

Ross and Kathryn Petras

**Andrews McMeel
Publishing**

Kansas City

www.andrewsmcmeel.com

98 99 00 01 02 • BIN • 10 9 8 7 6 5 4 3 2 1

Library of Congress Cataloging-in-Publication Data

Petras, Kathryn.
    Stupid celebrites : over 500 of the most idiotic things ever said by famous people / Kathryn Petras and Ross Petras.
        p.   cm.
    ISBN 0-8362-6837-7 (alk. paper)
    1. Celebrities—Quotations.   I. Petras, Ross   II. Title.
PN6084.C44P48   1998
081—dc21   98-22887
                                                                         CIP

Interior design by Scott Rattray

ATTENTION: SCHOOLS AND BUSINESSES

Andrews McMeel books are available at quantity discounts with bulk purchase for educational, business, or sales promotional use. For information, please write to: Special Sales Department, Andrews McMeel Publishing, 4520 Main Street, Kansas City, Missouri 64111.

STUPID CELEBRITIES

You CAN'T AVOID celebrities these days. They're on television, they're in magazines, they're writing books, they're all over the place. Some of us love them, some of us hate them, but we're all listening to them whether we like it or not.

And the more the celebrities talk, the higher the chances of something stupid coming out of their mouths. Something like:

> "Changing someone's life is not the best, is not wanting to change the other life. It is being who you are that changes another's life. Do you understand?"
>
> *actress Juliette Binoche*

Well, no, actually we don't. . . .

But we do know that statements like this deserve to be recognized. They deserve to live on and on. So, in the interest of preserving some not-so-great thoughts from so-great (and not-so-great) famous people, we put together this book. It's a collection of over five hundred of the most stupid comments from action movie stars, the idiotic utterances that drop from the lips of Oscar winners, the inane ravings of rock singers, and the generally stupid things everyone from Kate Winslet to Keanu Reeves to Quentin Tarantino to Kathie Lee Gifford to Courtney Love has been saying.

It includes:

- **Athletic Asininity:** Sports stars at their stupidest.

- **Supermodel Stupidity:** Revenge for those of us who aren't 5'11" and 110 pounds!

- **"Caught with Their Pants Down" Excuses:** The stupidest attempts to verbally wiggle out of tough situations.

- **Celebrities of the Past:** Proof that celebrities have been saying stupid things for years.

- **Politically Incorrect Babble:** Stone-age stupidity about women, about marriage, about almost anything . . .

- **Mogul Malaprops:** Syntactical excesses by titans of industry.

- **Not-So-Silver Tongues from the Silver Screen:** Miscues of speech and thought by some of the world's most famous actors.

All in all, *Stupid Celebrities* is a humorous celebration of the inevitable moment when someone famous puts their foot in their mouth.

It lets us see celebrities in those unguarded moments when the wrong thing slips out, when their thoughts get garbled and their tongues get twisted, and when they sound, well, kind of stupid. Of course that doesn't make them stupid; we *all* do it some of the time—but unlike the rest of us, when a celebrity makes a stupid misstatement, there's very often someone around with a microphone. And that's the gratifying thing about this book. It reminds us all that even though celebrities may be more famous than we are or more intelligent than we are or richer than we are, they don't always sound smarter than we do! Thank God for life's small consolations. . . .

We'd like to hear from you. . . .

If you have a favorite stupidity—celebrity or otherwise—that isn't in this book, send it to us. We're always looking for more stupid quotes. Please include a copy of your source or the date, time, and place where you heard it so we can verify it—and let us know if you want to be credited in print for your contribution. Contact us at:

Kathryn and Ross Petras
c/o Andrews McMeel Publishing
4520 Main Street
Kansas City, MO 64111-7701
or E-mail us at: stupidest@aol.com

And check out our web site: http//www.stupidest.com

STUPID
CELEBRITIES

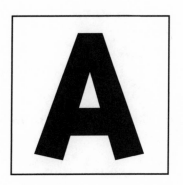

On Accomplishments, Ones to Brag about:

If I've made it a little easier for artists to work in violence, great! I've accomplished something.

> *director Quentin Tarentino, who directed such ultra-violent films as* Reservoir Dogs *and* Pulp Fiction

On Acting, Jean-Claude Van Damme's Interesting Insights on:

In an action film you act in the action. If it's a dramatic film you act in the drama.

> *action star Jean-Claude Van Damme, explaining his craft on* Lifestyles of the Rich and Famous

On Actors, a Bit Too Sensitive:

When I let up from the weed, and the drinking, too, I cried every day. And I *liked* that. I like crying. And now I not only wanna cry and show my crying to other people, I wanna just split myself down the middle and open my guts and just throw *everything* out!

> *actor Woody Harrelson*

On Actress/Models, Character Insights of:

I loved making *Rising Sun*. I got into the psychology of why she liked to get strangled and tied up in plastic bags. It has to do with low self-esteem.

actress/model Tatjana Patitz on her role in Rising Sun

On Adultery, Problems with Defining:

When you say I committed adultery, are you stating before the marriage of 1996 or prior to?

Dallas Cowboys cornerback Deion Sanders

On Aliases, Oh-So-Clever:

Mr. Donkey Penis

actor Johnny Depp's nom de plume at a hotel he checked into

On All-Star Games, Sexy:

It would take some of the lust off the All-Stars game.
> *Pete Rose discussing the then-only proposed idea of interleague baseball play*

On the Anals of History, Bottom Line about:

Also Sally Rose Lee is here. This name may go down in the anals of . . . anals . . . I believe that's *annals* . . .
> *Jay Leno, introducing a guest on* The Tonight Show

On Androgyny, Problems Understanding:

If I'm androgynous, I'd say I lean towards macho-androgynous.
> *actor John Travolta*

On Animal Rights, Deep Feelings about:

People don't know about the human part of me that really cares about the world. For instance, I don't know what I feel about wearing my furs anymore. I worked so hard to have a fur coat and I don't want to wear it anymore because I'm so wrapped up in the animals. I have real deep thoughts about it because I care about the world and nature.

singer Diana Ross

On the Art of the Deal, Early Signs of:

In the second grade . . . I punched my music teacher because I didn't think he knew much about music. . . . I'm not proud of that, but it's clear . . . that . . . early on I had a tendency to stand up.

mogul Donald Trump

On the Art of the Deal, Fascinating Facts about:

Deals work best when each side gets something it wants from the other.

mogul Donald Trump

On Asian Cities, Where Found:

Somewhere near Africa.
>*singer Barbra Streisand, telling Rosie O'Donnell where*
>*Rangoon—the capital of Burma aka Myanmar—was.*

On Asses, Important Acting Ability of:

Charlie Chaplin used his ass better than any other actor. In all of his films his ass is practically the protagonist. For a comic, the ass has incredible importance.
>*Italian actor Roberto Benigni*

On Autograph-Signing, Challenges with:

I'm still a little disconcerted when I'm asked to sign a lady's bosom. . . . It's a challenge to write one's name on a quivering breast without using the other hand to steady it.
>*Adam West, star of 1960s* Batman, *in his autobiography*
>Back to the Batcave

On Ax Murderers, Yucky:

There is an ax murderer inside me. Yessir. She's frightful, gruesome, green, and slimy.

actress Sally Field

On Band Leaders, Tinkling:

We have to take a break, because I can see Billy is about to tinkle again.

> *talk show host David Frost, trying to say that his bandleader was about to play music*

On Barbara Walters, Reasons to Watch:

I'm a big fan of hers. She's a sexy woman. Got great t--s, and she's a really good-looking old broad.

> *talk show host Geraldo Rivera on newsperson Barbara Walters*

On Baseball Team Ownership, Handy Hints about:

I used to be very hands-on, but lately I've been more hands-off and I plan to become more hands-on and less hands-off and hope that hands-on will become better than hands-off, the way hands-on used to be.

> *New York Yankees owner George Steinbrenner explaining his view on team ownership*

On *Baywatch*, Brainy Stars of:

Reporter: Did you realize you have five gold albums in Germany and Austria?
Actor David Hasselhoff: Where's Austria?
        attributed to David Hasselhoff, star of Baywatch *and*
        Baywatch Nights, *whose songs sell very well in Europe*

On *Baywatch*, Why David Hasselhoff Believes It's the Plots and Morals People Are Watching:

I went in and said, "If I see one more gratuitous shot of a woman's body, I'm quitting. . . . " I think the show should be emotional story lines, morals, real-life heroes. And that's what we're doing. . . .
        David Hasselhoff, star of T&A hit Baywatch

On Baywatch, Why We Should Be Thankful for It:

Beyond its entertainment value, *Baywatch* has enriched and, in many cases, helped save lives. I'm looking forward to the opportunity to continue with a project which has had such significance for so many.
        actor David Hasselhoff

On Beauty Queens, Self-Image of:

People are waiting for a political leader, a messiah.

> *1997 Miss Universe Irene Saez on her plans to run for President of Venezuela*

On Being a Man, a Man:

I'm not sitting around depressed, going, "Oh, people are going to think I'm not Eddie anymore. I'm not a man." I know I'm a man. I'm a man.

> *actor Eddie Murphy, after being pulled over for picking up a transvestite*

On Being a Mess, Great Philosophical Observations on:

. . . I am a mess and you're a mess, too. Everyone's a mess. Which means, actually, that no one's a mess. Know what I mean?

> *singer Fiona Apple in an interview*

On Being a Mess, Greatness of:

I read biographies of the greats, and they were so messed up that I thought I'd better mess myself up. But I couldn't. I'm too small.
actress Winona Ryder

On Being Asked about the Parthenon:

Reporter: Did you visit the Parthenon during your trip to Greece?
Shaquille O'Neal: I can't really remember the names of the clubs that we went to.

On Being Blown Up, Happy Thoughts about:

The reward of not having children [is] if I get blown up tomorrow, I'll have lived long enough and I won't have to worry about my children.
Cosmopolitan *magazine founder Helen Gurley Brown*

On Being Killed, Surprising Facts about:

Smoking kills. If you're killed, you've lost a very important part of your life.

> *actress Brooke Shields, demonstrating why she should*
> *become spokesperson for a federal antismoking campaign*

On Being Thin

If she wasn't so skinny, she'd be considered thin.
> *director Gregory Ratoff*

On Bisexuals, Unusual Body Parts of:

A lot of my peer group think I'm an eccentric bisexual, like I may even have an ammonia-filled tentacle or something somewhere on my body. That's okay.
> *actor Robert Downey Jr.*

On Bitches and German Dictators, Logical Connection between:

I know a lot of women who use men, but the world is not perfect. Fifty years ago there was Hitler; now there are bitches everywhere.
actress Julie Delpy

On Bizarre Self-Assessment, Action Film Stars and:

I'm the Hiroshima of love.
actor Sylvester Stallone

On Blondness, Horrible Effects of:

Being a blond makes you very ruthless, insane, and self-centered.
actress Sean Young on wearing a blond wig in
Fatal Instinct

On Blonds versus Brunettes, the Final Word on:

When you get a truly mean, evil woman who is blond, she's always meaner than a brunette. You have to divide blonds into the fair blonds and the honey blonds. . . . The honey blonds are never evil and the pale blonds are always troublesome.
writer Norman Mailer

On Blossoming Sexual Creatures:

In college I slept with a couple of guys, like we all do, and a couple of girls, like we all do. Then I got to New York City and I just blossomed into this sexual creature.
actress Linda Fiorentino

On Boasts, Proud:

When we measured heads in eighth grade, mine was the biggest.
actress Marilu Henner

On the Bogeyman, Grown-Up Thoughts about:

I do have odd habits. I check under my bed every night for the bogeyman. That's just a little thing, though.

actress Tori Spelling

On Bonding Films:

. . . this [*Dances With Wolves*] is a bonding film for all. You could put it anywhere in history—the Berlin Wall, Kuwait.

actor Kevin Costner

On Books, Good to Have:

We have to buy a lot of books. I really respect books.

mogul Donald Trump on his empty bookshelves in his new Trump Tower penthouse

On Boring Men, Madonna's Humanity Toward:

I live for meetings with men in suits. I love them because I know they had a really boring week and I walk in there with my orange velvet leggings and drop popcorn in my cleavage and then fish it out and eat it. I like that. I know I'm entertaining them, and I know that they know.

pop star Madonna

On Boxers, Big Words and:

Woman: You're a pugilist, aren't you?
World champ boxer Rocky Graziano: Nah, I'm just a prizefighter.

On Boxing Promoters, Punchy New Words from:

I have come up with a word to describe Trump: telesynergistic. That means, "progress ingeniously planned by geometric progression— the capability of transforming dreams into living reality, in minimal time, at megaprofits."

boxing promoter Don King on Donald Trump

On Breaking Up Is Hard to Do, Sensitive Actors and:

You buy a bad car, it breaks down, what are you gonna do?
actor Charlie Sheen on breaking up with model
Donna Peele

On Breaking Up, Sensitive Thoughts about:

I've always been the one to push and shove and say, "Sorry, that's it darlin', it's all over, goodbye. Take twenty Valiums and have a stomach pump and that's the end of it."
singer Rod Stewart

On Breasts, Career Value of:

I consider [Madonna] a friend, and she sure knows how to work that publicity machine. Of course, I don't have breasts. If I did have, I'd be in the number one spot over Madonna.
director Spike Lee

On Breasts, Final Word on:

When they're huge, you become very self-conscious. . . . I've learned something, though, through my years of pondering and pontificating, and that is: Men love them, and I love that.

actress Drew Barrymore

On Brooke Shields, Personal Finance and:

I'm so naive about finances. Once when my mother mentioned an amount and I realized I didn't understand she had to explain: "That's like three Mercedes." Then I understood.

actress Brooke Shields

On Bryant Gumbel, Life of the Party:

It's not that I dislike many people. It's just that I don't like many people.

TV newsperson Bryant Gumbel

On Butt Shots, Excellent Reasons for:

People talk about my pictures. So long as they continue talking about butts, they will not be killing each other.

> *Yoko Ono, discussing an innovative art project she was showing in Langenhagen, Germany—posters of unidentified buttocks*

On Career Choices, Careful:

Because modeling is lucrative, I'm able to save up and be more particular about the acting roles I take.

> *attributed to model-actress Kathy Ireland, star of*
> *Hollywood movies like* Alien from L.A. *and* Danger Island

On Career Choices, God-Given:

It was God who made me so beautiful. If I weren't, then I'd be a teacher.

> *supermodel Linda Evangelista*

On Catfights:

She had a tit job for sure. This is desperation. Well, maybe she'll get a job out of it.

> *pop star Madonna on La Toya Jackson's appearance in* Playboy

Madonna is a no-talent. She slept with everybody on the way up. That's how she made it to the top.

> *singer La Toya Jackson's reply*

On Chairs, Hairy:

When I see the pictures you play in that theater, it makes the hair stand on the edge of my seat.
director Michael Curtiz

On Chances, Wild:

Histrionics are against him.
TV announcer John Tesh, on a gymnast's chances for an Olympic medal

On Charities for the Ugly, Dolly Parton's Contributions to:

I believe in my cosmetics line. There are plenty of charities for the homeless. Isn't it time somebody helped the homely?
singer Dolly Parton

On Charity, Good Reasons Not to Give to:

We're young and we need the money to build and do more.
Ivana Trump explaining why she and Donald didn't give much to charity

On Charity, Hollywood-Style:

Charity is taking an ugly girl to lunch.
actor Warren Beatty

On Cheating, the French Definition of:

I think a man can have two, maybe three affairs, while he is married. But three is the absolute maximum. After that, you're cheating.
actor Yves Montand

On Cheese:

No! No! I don't want cheese! I can't see cheese! I can't eat cheese! I'm allergic to cheese!

> *Televangelist Reverend Robert Schuller, who got upset when an airline flight attendant tried to serve him cheese. Schuller then reportedly demanded all the grapes on the flight instead of cheese.*

On Chicago, the Fifty-Second State:

I was asked to come to Chicago because Chicago is one of our fifty-two states.

> *actress Raquel Welch, on her appearance at a pro-choice rally in Chicago, on* Larry King Live

On Chicken McNuggets, Sad Facts about:

A Chicken McNugget doesn't die any easier than baby fur seals, and the fact that somebody could be so insipid as to think that the chicken has less rights than the baby fur seal because it's not as cute can kiss my ass.

rocker Ted Nugent

On Chicks:

There's something you get from a chick that you can't have with any other being on the planet, and that is something super special. I mean, if there were nothing but old whores and nasty, old, hard women, I'd be out looking for some young, sweet, little fifteen-year-old boy.

actor Don Johnson

On Children, Good Reasons Not to Have:

No, no. What if they were not as good as me? What would I do with those imbeciles?

> *dancer Rudolf Nureyev telling Morley Safer why he didn't want children*

On Choices, Difficult:

You can have either the Resurrection or you can have Liberace. But you can't have both.

> *performer Liberace when told his show was being billed with the Easter show at Radio City Music Hall*

On Choosing a Mate, Horse Sense and:

It's like when I buy a horse. I don't want a thick neck and short legs.

> *actor Mickey Rourke describing what he wants in a woman*

On Chutzpah, Excessive:

Reporter (in front of Russian sign): Are you having any trouble with the Russian language?
Newscaster Connie Chung: Not at all.
Reporter: Well, then, why are you standing in the men's room?

On *Citizen Kane,* Competition for:

I hate tooting my own horn, but after Steven [Spielberg] saw *Yentl,* he said, "I wish I could tell you how to fix your picture, but I can't. It's the best film I've seen since *Citizen Kane.*

actress Barbra Streisand

On *Citizen Kane,* More Competition for:

I've made some great ones. *Risky Business* still stands up. It's timeless. They study that film in film school.

actress Rebecca DeMornay

On Cities, Stately:

Every city I go to is an opportunity to paint, whether it's Omaha or Hawaii.

singer Tony Bennett

On Civil Rights Workers, Tireless:

I look at [modeling] as something I'm doing for black people in general.

model Naomi Campbell

On Clarity, Bill Parcells and:

Concentration-wise, we're having trouble crossing the line mentally from a toughness standpoint.

New England Patriots coach Bill Parcells, after the Patriots lost to Houston

On the Classics, Mike Tyson and:

When I was in prison I was wrapped up in all those deep books. That Tolstoy crap. People shouldn't read that stuff.

boxer Mike Tyson on what he read before he decided he preferred comic books

On the Classics, Religious:

It's a great little book.

actress Sean Young, on the Bible

On the Classics, Sylvester Stallone and:

I'm astounded by people who take eighteen years to write something. That's how long it took that guy to write *Madame Bovary,* and was that ever on the best-seller list?

actor Sylvester Stallone

On Clear Statements, Actresses and:

Changing someone's life is not the best, is not wanting to change the other life. It is being who you are that changes another's life. Do you understand?

actress Juliette Binoche

On Clear Thinking, Winona Ryder and:

I reached a crescendo in my life where I was, mmm . . . not in a good place. I thought in some way to be a good actress I had to be in a lot of pain. Then it occurred to me that I didn't. I was actually a better actress when I had a life to return to and I could sleep at night. That came from working with people like Meryl Streep on *House of the Spirits,* who can go home at night and also be Meryl Streep and be brilliant. I didn't know that. When you grow up acting you watch your heroes and think they must be in pain to be that good. Actually that's very ridiculous.

actress Winona Ryder

On Coeducation, Why It's So Nice:

It's nice; it gives you a feeling of security so that if something breaks we know we can always call a guy over and he'll bring a drill or something.

actress Brooke Shields when she was a college student
explaining why it was good to have men in a dorm

On Cold Endurance Ability, *Baywatch* Superstar and:

We've all had hypothermia at times. David Charvet almost had to be hospitalized. But it's easier for me to endure the cold because I'm an owner of the show and I'm the highest-paid guy.
actor David Hasselhoff

On Commercial Breaks, Great Moments in:

We'll be right back after this word from General Fools.
former Good Morning America *host David Hartman*

On Compliments, Very, Very Pretentious:

Andre Agassi is very, very intelligent, very, very sensitive, very evolved more than his linear years.
singer Barbra Streisand

On Computer Billionaires, Infallibility of:

640K ought to be enough for anybody.
attributed to Bill Gates, Microsoft CEO, back in 1981

On Conclusions, Amazing:

Everywhere I went, my cleavage followed. But I learned I am not my cleavage.
attributed to model Carole Mallory

On Confessions, Thrilling:

I don't have any underwear on tonight.
Sally Kirkland during 1994 Oscar ceremony to a reporter

On Congressman Gopher, PC-ness of:

We're going to put you back in the fashion department.
>*Congressperson Fred Grandy, formerly "Gopher" on TV's*
>The Love Boat, *answering a question from a female reporter*

On Conservatives, Kinky:

Joey Bishop, talk show host: Would you like to become a regular on the show?
Senator Barry Goldwater: No, thank you. I'd much rather watch you in bed with my wife.

On Conversational Topics, Seasonal:

I only talk about the weather in season.
>*director Gregory Ratoff*

On Cooking, Not-So-Helpful Hints in:

Then you add two forkfuls of cooking oil . . .
>*chef Julia Child in her famous TV cooking show,*
The French Chef

On Corporations, Why They're Fun:

Corporately, we believe in orgasms.
>*NBC Entertainment president Warren Littlefield on why
he's proud of women discussing their sex lives on an NBC
TV show*

On Cosmic Reactions:

My reaction was very immediate and shocking. I looked down at the floor and I saw his shoes, and I loved his shoes. Then I was double in love with him. His shoes were camel-color, and my cosmic thoughts were like, "Those are camels, and I'd trek across any desert to follow."

>*actress Drew Barrymore*

On Cosmo Girls, Frightening Thoughts from:

There aren't enough men to go around. . . . Every time there's a plane accident, it's one hundred men dead . . . and I literally think, "Why couldn't some women have been on that flight?"

Cosmopolitan *magazine founder Helen Gurley Brown*

On Countdowns, Unusual:

87, 79, 78, 70, 69 . . .

actor Tim Allen (as quoted in Newsweek*) failing a sobriety test in June 1997 when asked to count backward from eighty-seven after being stopped for speeding. He pleaded not guilty.*

On Counting Words, Donald Trump and:

I'll tell you, it's Big Business. If there is one word to describe Atlantic City, it's Big Business. Or two words—Big Business.

Donald Trump, real estate tycoon, looking down on Atlantic City from his helicopter, as quoted in a 1989 Time

On Courage under . . . Shooting:

They were doing a full back shot of me in a swimsuit and I thought, oh my God, I have to be so brave. See, every woman hates herself from behind.

attributed to model Cindy Crawford

On Critics, What They Do:

We hate critics. . . . Most of them are fat and ugly and they criticize.
Milli Vanilli, Grammy-winning group later criticized for allegedly lip-synching to songs recorded by others

On Crotches, Importance in Acting of:

I act from my crotch. That's where my force is. Sexuality is my strongest driving force and as I get older and older, I find it is less and less, shall we say, compelling.

actor Jeremy Irons

On Cruel and Unusual Punishment, Televangelists and:

They made him bend over in front of all those men.
>*former televangelist Tammy Faye Bakker on her husband Jim being strip-searched during the 1980s sex scandal*

On Cubism and Noses, Tempting Arguments:

One is tempted to argue that cubism grew out of the inside of the nose, for, indeed, its interior is often a cavernous, clotted, intricate web, full of bogs, stalactites, stalagmites, filamentlike hairs.
>*writer Norman Mailer in* Portrait of Picasso as a
>Young Man

On Cult Suicides, Dubious Comments about:

There are too many nuts running around anyway, right? It's a good way to get rid of a few nuts, you know, you gotta look at it that way.
>*cable TV mogul Ted Turner, expressing his opinion of the Heaven's Gate cult suicide*

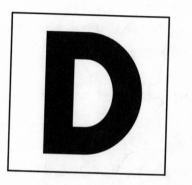

On Dads, Enlightened:

I finally got it right.

> *actor Jack Nicholson, in 1992, on hearing of the birth of his son after having had two daughters*

On Dads, In-the-Know:

It seemed that my wife Shirley was always pregnant until we found out what was causing it.

> *singer Pat Boone, explaining why his wife didn't travel with him*

On Dads-to-Be, Thoughtful:

Even when Alana was seven or eight months pregnant, I was still getting her to wear short skirts and high-heeled shoes. Actually, I did that to Kelly, too, but Kelly's a lot younger and she didn't mind.

> *singer Rod Stewart on his relationships with Alana Hamilton and Kelly Emberg while they were pregnant*

On the Dangerous Derek Parents:

My parents were beautiful and they believed that anyone who wasn't should be put to sleep. I know what to do with beauty.
producer/director John Derek

On Dates, Ones We Don't Want to Go on:

. . . my philosophy of dating is to just fart right away.
TV personality Jenny McCarthy in her book, Jen-X

On Dates with Mick Jagger, What You Talk about:

Mick Jagger and I just really liked each other a lot. We talked all night. We had the same views on nuclear disarmament.
model Jerry Hall talking about how she met her husband, rock star Mick Jagger

On Dating, Metaphorical Millionaire's Thoughts about:

Germ phobia is a problem. You have to be selective. It's pretty dangerous out there. It's like Vietnam! Dating is my personal Vietnam!
mogul Donald Trump on the Howard Stern Show

On Dating, Spago Considerations in:

Can you imagine me with a woman old enough to be my wife? No, really, I'm serious. Can you imagine me walking into Spago with a seventy-year-old woman? Forget it. F--- that! I don't have the spirit. My girlfriend is twenty-five years old; perfect.
actor Tony Curtis on his relationship with a woman forty-six years younger than himself

On David Bowie, Insufferability of:

At the risk of sounding pompous, I guess I would align it [playing with Tin Machine in 1991] with deconstructionism. The point made by the French in the Sixties that we are working our way towards a society that is deeply involved with hybridization and contradictory information almost to the point where contradiction simply ceases to exist . . .

> *singer David Bowie, after first explaining how his time with Tin Machine put him "in flux as far as public perception was concerned . . . that hard-lined Appolonian thing around me had broken down."*

On Dead People, Fun:

Sure the body count in this movie bothers me, but what are you gonna do? It's what everybody likes. At least it's not an awful body count—it's a fun body count.

> *actress Bonnie Bedelia, star of* Die Harder, *in a* Movies USA *interview*

On Death, Important Thoughts on:

If you have intercourse you run the risk of dying and the ramifications of death are final.

> *singer Cyndi Lauper, during an MTV interview*

On Decade Differentiation, Donald Trump and:

The 1990s sure aren't like the 1980s.
mogul Donald Trump

On Decision Making:

Reporter: Would you quit baseball if the Yankees lose the series to the Pirates?
Casey Stengel, then New York Yankees manager: Well, I have given that thought a lot of thinking lately and last night, well—I finally made up my mind.
Reporter: Which way?
Stengel: I made up my mind both ways.
Casey Stengel, at a press conference before a decisive World Series game

On Decisiveness:

So basically, I don't know what I'm talking about. But maybe I do.
TV personality Jenny McCarthy in her book, Jen-X

On Deep Statements, Movie Star-Style:

I don't want to be anyone else these days, but everybody wears masks. Wouldn't it be cool if we could just be ourselves?
> *actor Jim Carrey, in an interview following his role in* The Mask

On Deep Thoughts, Where to Have:

I was thinking about dying the other day. . . . The death thought came while I was sitting on my toilet peeing—that's where I have my most contemplative thoughts.
> *pop star Madonna, in* Madonna—The Book

On Describing Harmonicas, Great Moments in:

It's about four to five inches long and you blow it . . . oh my God!
> *actress June Lockhart trying to describe a harmonica on a quiz show*

On Dieting, Key Distinctions about:

I don't diet. I just don't eat as much as I'd like to.
        supermodel Linda Evangelista

On Differences:

We have no differences because we have nothing in common.
        tennis player Guillermo Vilas speaking about Argentina
        Davis Cup teammate Jose Luis Clerc

On Diplomatic Questions, Vital:

They say you have to stop eating when he does. But what if he's
having a snack and you're starving? Do you have to eat fast?
        basketball superstar Charles Barkley, member of the US
        Olympic Basketball Team, on being introduced to Prince
        Rainier of Monaco

On Directional Confusion, Cher and:

I've been up and down so many times that I feel as if I'm in a revolving door.

actress Cher

On Directors, Typical:

This is a terrific script. It just needs a complete rewrite.

director Peter Bogdanovich to screenwriter Alvin Sargent, after reading a draft of Paper Moon

On Disco Music, God and:

God had to create disco music so that I could be born and be successful.

singer Donna Summer

On Dishwashing, Important Insights about:

I know that if you leave dishes in the sink, they get sticky and hard to wash the next day.

>*actor/body builder Arnold Schwarzenegger*

On Distinctions, Crucial:

It's a hairweave.

>*shamed sportscaster Marv Albert when asked by Barbara Walters if he wears a toupee*

On Divorce, the Positive Capitalist Side of:

It's really pretty sad, but it's been great for business.

>*mogul Donald Trump on the publicity around his split with Ivana*

On Dogs, Mugly

I've never seen black men with fine white women. They be ugly, mugly dogs. And you always see white men with good-looking black women.

director Spike Lee

On Dogs, Similarity to Women and:

Women are great. When they dig you, there's nothing they won't do. That kind of loyalty is hard to find—unless you've got a good dog.

rock singer David Lee Roth

On Donald Trump, Star Creator:

I love creating stars. To some extent I have done that with Ivana. To a certain extent I have done that with Marla. I have really given a lot of women great opportunity. Unfortunately, after they are a star, the fun is over for me.

mogul Donald Trump

On Drag Queens, Liquid:

RuPaul is a boundless energy that can pour itself into whatever shape it wants.

drag star RuPaul

On Drew Barrymore, Cosmic Thoughts from:

People talk from the heart, the mind, the body. They never talk about the tummy. The tummy tells a lot.

actress Drew Barrymore

On Ears, Why to Bite:

This is my career. I have children to raise. I have to retaliate.
boxer Mike Tyson explaining why he bit Evander Holyfield's
ear after Holyfield head-butted him

On Ego:

I think of my secret of success as being that I never was a pretentious person.
talk show host Geraldo Rivera

On Egos, Colossal:

It sounds vain, but I could probably make a difference for almost everyone I ever met if I chose to involve myself with them either professionally or personally.
actor Kevin Costner

On Egos, Maybe a Bit Overinflated:

It's tough. For me, the problem is looking good all the time. People say "Know who I saw today? Sydney Biddle Barrows! And she looked awful!" Because for most people, you're the high point in their life.

"Mayflower Madam" Sydney Biddle Barrows

On Elvis, What Really Happened to Him:

They say Elvis is dead. He's not dead. He's just a different color. He's 6 foot 8 inches, 225 pounds, plays basketball, and he's black.

basketball player Dennis Rodman to USA Today

On Elvis Has Just Left the White House:

If it hadn't been for his tragic and untimely death, the king of rock 'n' roll might be sitting in the Oval Office today.

The National Enquirer *on Elvis, who, they report, was being groomed for political office by Richard Nixon*

On E-Mail Addresses, In-the-Know Hollywood Ways of Describing:

I have his Internet number.
> *actress Sandra Bullock, as a purported computer whiz, in* The Net

On Empathy, Martha Stewart's Amazing:

I'm trying to tell people I don't want to hear that anymore. That's your own problem. You have to figure it out yourself. I have.
> *Martha Stewart at a charity luncheon responding to a remark that most women feel inadequate to handle the demands of their lives*

On the Environment, Deep Thoughts about:

[The movie *Amazon*] takes place in the Amazon and what you realize is that this man has to make major choices, and he makes major mistakes instead of the right things, and through his mistakes he learns a lot of soulful things, and he actually corrects his inner life, which, of course, helps enhance his outer life, and through the whole process we learn about how sad it is that we have something called the Amazon forest and we're destroying it, and yet I say as an American-Canadian actress, it's sad what we're doing to [forests] in America.

actress Rae Dawn Chong

On Etiquette, Rock Stars and:

Afterward she thinks she's staying the night. I politely ask her to leave. She gets upset. I give her five minutes and then throw her clothes just outside the door. She opens the door and leans to pick them up. I kick her out and phone security to tell them there's a naked woman knocking on my door.

member of rock group UB40 describing how he gets rid of groupies

On Existential Thoughts, Keanu Reeves-Style:

I guess I'm not really involving my imagination to that of a circumstance or happening—I'm just kind of acknowledging it as an existence.

> *actor Keanu Reeves, when reminded that the Art Center College of Design in Pasadena, California, was offering a Keanu Reeves film class*

On Explanations, Dubious:

I was trying to make fun—there were 150 people outside, the audience was screaming. You know I was going, "Uuuuh. . . ." I couldn't think of the word "embankment" and then I looked at the backdrop. I would do anything but talk about what I contractually had to do, which was talk about *Playboy*—I wasn't comfortable doing it—you know, I did it with Johnny Carson.

> *actress Farrah Fawcett explaining why she was incoherent when she appeared on David Letterman's show*

On the Eyes, Importance of:

I think every woman ought to wear eyelashes, because I think the eyes are such an important part of the face.

> *former televangelist Tammy Faye Bakker in* Christian Wives, *explaining that she always wears lots of makeup to bed*

On Eyes, Prehistoric:

I had just gone to see my anthropologist and he dilated my eyes.

> *actress Shelley Winters explaining why she had fallen off a curb in Santa Monica*

On Facts, Frightening:

Baywatch will be *their* [foreign audience's] concept of what America is!

> actor David Hasselhoff, star of Baywatch, *which is seen in 140 different countries by over one billion people*

On Fame, Coo-Coo:

Come on, George. Loosen up. Swing, man. Dust off those gossamer wings and fly yourself to the moon of your choice and be grateful to carry the baggage we've all had to carry. . . . You're top dog on the top rung of a ladder called Stardom, which in Latin means thanks-to-the-fans who were there when it was lonely.

> *singer Frank Sinatra in a letter in the* Los Angeles Times *to singer George Michael who had said he was unhappy about fame*

On Famous Last Words:

Cheating is out of the question. Sure, Frank sees sexy flight attendants and business women when he flies around the country. But the only come-on he gets anymore is, "C'mon, Frank, show us a picture of Cody."

TV talk show host Kathie Lee Gifford in her book I Can't Believe I Said That

On Fans, a Bit Overenthusiastic:

If he were here, I'd ask him if I could lick his eyeballs.
actor Christian Slater on being a fan of Jack Nicholsons

On Farm Life, Kinky:

It's terrific to have a woman in your life who feeds the chickens while wearing one of your shirts, black underwear and stiletto heels.
actor Peter Strauss

On Fascinating Thoughts, Marlon Brando and:

The most repulsive thing you could ever imagine is the inside of a camel's mouth. That and watching a girl eat octopus or squid.
actor Marlon Brando

On Fashion Designers, Logical Fears of:

I hate them. They are so dangerous. Marie Antoinette had her bedroom covered in peacock feathers and look how badly she ended.
designer Karl Lagerfeld on why he won't use peacock feathers

On Fashion Designers, Philosophical Thoughts of:

We are all looking at how we have to shift, because you look at the good and you look at what's not working, and I think people, God bless it, are working in the consciousness, God bless it, that with all the problems out there in the world, how are we going to shift the consciousness?
designer Donna Karan, devout follower of New Age guru Deepak Chopra, expounding upon her philosophical and spiritual beliefs

On Fashion Photographers, Wholesome Habits of:

I always carry chains in the trunk of my car because you never know when you'll need them. You know, you go out in the streets in Paris and you might want to chain a model to a fence.

photographer Helmut Newton

On Fashion Shows, Intellectual Drama of:

What truly surprised and satisfied me when I did my first show for John Galliano is how he explains every moment of the event. He comes to each of us individually to tell us about the part we're supposed to play when we show his beautiful creations. Just like for a play. For example, for a dress that was inspired by a storm or by anger, I have to imagine I'm playing the part of Scarlett O'Hara in *Gone with the Wind.*

model Kate Moss

On Fatness, Non-Fatness of:

It is not fatness. It is *development.*
  actress Anita Ekberg explaining why she didn't need to diet
  even though she had gained weight

On Fatherhood, Noble:

I had to make this choice between Tatum and this girl—and I chose Farrah. Tatum made me choose. I said, "That's a bad idea. I sleep with this girl, Tatum. I don't sleep with you."
  actor Ryan O'Neal talking about his daughter, Tatum, and
  future wife, Farrah Fawcett

On Fatherhood, Temporary:

TV variety show host Ed Sullivan: Wasn't Alan Jones your father?
Singer Jack Jones: He still is.

On Faxing, Leeza Gibbon's Understanding of:

We want to hear your story. Call us or fax us your video.
talk show host Leeza Gibbons, asking for contributions during her Leeza *talk show*

On Feeling Good, When It Happens:

I feel my best when I'm happy.
actress Winona Ryder

On Femaleness:

Femaleness is at least as powerful as maleness. But it's rare, y'know.
singer Ann Wilson of rock band Heart

On Feminism, Charles Barkley and:

Listening to a woman is almost as bad as losing to one. There are only three things that women are better at than men: cleaning, cooking, and having sex.
basketball superstar Charles Barkley

On Feminist Chicks, Boy-Girl Society and:

These chicks are our natural enemy. . . . It is time to do battle with them. . . . What I want is a devastating piece that takes the militant feminists apart. [They are] unalterably opposed to the romantic boy-girl society that *Playboy* promotes.

   Playboy *publisher Hugh Hefner in an interoffice memo*

On Fifteen, Fifteenness of:

By the time I was your age, I was fifteen!
   director Michael Curtiz scolding a child star

On Fifteen-Minute Celebrities, Brain Power of:

There's been so much media about me being a surfer dude and a lot of other jobs. I guess it's time to prove myself, to let the people know, heck, I've a brain.

  O. J. Simpson's houseguest Kato Kaelin

On Films about Strippers, What They're Not about, Part One:

You know what—dancing, and nudity was not what this movie was about.

> *actor Bruce Willis, at the New York premiere of* Striptease, *the movie in which his wife dances naked for men*

On Films about Strippers, What They're Not about, Part Two:

It's not really about taking your clothes off.
> *actress Demi Moore*

On Films about Strippers, What They're *Really* about:

It's a spiritual message. And, forgive me, but I think it's almost a deeply religious message on a very personal level.

> *screenwriter Joe Eszterhaus, commenting on his film flop* Showgirls, *which chronicled the travails of an exotic dancer in Las Vegas who wanted to be a legit showgirl*

On Financial Responsibility, Great Moments in:

It [money] was put in my checking account for me and I just spent it, and when it was gone, I waited for next week. All I know is I got it and I spent it like any woman would.

former televangelist Tammy Faye Bakker on money

On First Impressions, Odd:

He reminded me of an alien.

actress Kelly LeBrock on first meeting Steven Seagal, who later became her husband . . . then her ex-husband

On Fit Parents, Woody Allen and:

I don't have to be there when the diapers are changed or anything really awful happens.

director Woody Allen on raising Mia Farrow's children

On Football, Amazing:

Football is an incredible game. Sometimes it's so incredible, it's unbelievable.

> *Dallas Cowboys coach Tom Landry*

On Frank Sinatra, Geopolitical Charm and:

Go back to China!

> *singer Frank Sinatra to a female South Korean blackjack dealer in Las Vegas who wasn't setting the cards up the way he liked them*

On Frank Sinatra, Golf versus Human Rights and:

I'll go anywhere I wanna go, anytime I wanna go. I had a great time. They had a great golf course.

> *singer Frank Sinatra on his visit to South Africa while it was still under white apartheid rule*

On Freedom, Losing Your Head about:

The only luxury is freedom, freedom of the mind. They can chop off my head and take everything else as long as they leave me that.
Dieter Meier, of the rock group Yello

On Freudian Slips:

This is a work of fiction that reads like nonfiction.
O. J. Simpson "Dream Team" lawyer Robert Shapiro commenting on his own book, The Search for Justice. *After saying this, he quickly corrected himself, explaining that he meant to say just the opposite.*

On Friendly Banter on Morning Shows, Freudian Slips and:

Think springtime, Bryant. Four more days and the little croci will begin to poke their heads up your shorts.
TV weatherman Willard Scott to Bryant Gumbel on The Today Show

On Fun:

I enjoy getting dressed as a Barbie doll.
TV spokesmodel Vanna White

On Fur Coats, Philosophical Questions about:

I believe that mink are raised for being turned into fur coats and if we didn't wear fur coats those little animals would never have been born. So is it better not to have been born or to have lived for a year or two to have been turned into a fur coat? I don't know.
Barbi Benton, ex-Playboy bunny turned actress

On the Future, Facts about:

There's no stopping the future.
baseball great Yogi Berra

On the Future, More of It:

There is certainly more in the future now than back in 1964.
rocker Roger Daltrey

On Game Shows, Great Moments in:

Show me another nipple and I'll give you $200.
> *Let's Make a Deal game show host Monty Hall, to a woman in the audience who held up a baby bottle*

On Gay Rights, Former Orange Juice Spokesperson's Odd Views on:

If gays are granted rights, next we'll have to give rights to prostitutes and to people who sleep with St. Bernards and to nailbiters.
> *singer and former spokesperson for Florida orange juice Anita Bryant*

On Generalizations, Surprising:

That man is so repugnant. All of these satanic murderers are.
> *talk show host Geraldo Rivera discussing Charles Manson*

On Genetics, the Scary Truth about:

You used to get up in the morning and you'd pick up your weaponry and you'd walk. Maybe you'd run a little bit. You'd hunt and you'd kill. You'd come back and on your way back you'd eat some vegetables. And then you'd f--k. And if she didn't want to f--k, you'd make her. And if she still didn't, you'd kill her. And then you'd eat what you brought back and share it with whoever did f--k you and then you'd sleep a little bit. And get up. And then you'd go do it again. There's a lot of that stuff that's in our genetics.

    actor Sean Penn

On Genius:

The world "genius" isn't applicable in football. A genius is a guy like Norman Einstein.

> *Joe Theisman, ESPN broadcaster and ex-Redskins quarterback (Theisman later explained to* Sports Illustrated *that this was no error; he was referring to a high school classmate of his, Norman Einstein, who graduated at the top of his class.)*

On Geography:

Person: The Japanese have destroyed Pearl Harbor!
Actress Joan Crawford: Oh dear, who was she?

On George Eliot, Perky TV Talk Show Host's Knowledge of:

I love all of his books.
> *talk show host Kathie Lee Gifford to an actor appearing in George Eliot's* Middlemarch. *Unfortunately, George Eliot was the pen name for writer—and woman—Mary Ann Evans.*

On Geometric Acting:

I got to do some stuff in it that was . . . that was bitchin'. Like, the physical aspect of the character and its portrayal. I was doing really precise, straight lines. Investigating that shape with emotion. I was doing a whole thing of, like, mother equals round. Anger equals straight. I saw the heart as a round notion. The journey of this character starts out very angular and straight. By breaking him down compassion is born. And he gains responsibility and compassion and a warming. Then he's open for an embrace.

actor Keanu Reeves

On Getting Eaten by Crocodiles, Thoughts about:

I'm obsessed with crocodiles and getting eaten by one. When I hear that someone's been eaten by a crocodile or shark, I just get all gooey. I start salivating.

singer Tori Amos as quoted in Rolling Stone

On Getting Tattooed, the Sheer Exhilaration of:

I let him do it. And it felt so good. God, that pain is like nothing else in the world. And it's so sexual, too, you know? I mean, after it's done you just want to go and drive a car off a cliff or something, you know?

actress Drew Barrymore after getting a tattoo

On Ghosts, Savvy:

I'd been thinking about the Nike ad all day. I immediately understood what he was telling me.

> *singer Michael Jackson explaining that he had sold John Lennon's song "Revolution" to Nike because Lennon's ghost told him to "Let my music live"*

On Gigs, Moving:

We were in Milwaukee playing the Metalfest. We're a folk band—we should not have been there. They threw beer at us and told us to f--k off. It was beautiful.

> *actor Keanu Reeves, on his band Dogstar*

On Girlfriends, Heavy:

I had a girlfriend, but I got that piano off my back.

> *actor Charlie Sheen*

On Goals, Easy to Achieve:

My main hope for myself is to be where I am.
actor Woody Harrelson

On Goals, Hard to Achieve:

At that point, my peers were all gay male dancers. I wanted to be accepted. I wanted to be a gay male dancer.
actress Carrie Fisher, on being a teenager in Las Vegas

On Goals, Worthwhile:

The movie I do could be like my photo layouts, where I look like I've just been raped or I'm being raped. . . . I can't wait to be abused in a film. It's some fantasy that's burning inside of me.
model Charlotte Lewis

On Golf, Freudian Slips and:

I've got balls older than that.

> *Bob Hope during a golf tournament, to a pretty Desert Classic woman who told him she was twenty-four. He meant golf balls.*

On God, So Cool:

[God's] like, so cool. Think of the coolest person in your life. He made that person. And *He's* cooler than *that*.

> *actress Justine Bateman*

On Godzilla, Political Awareness of:

What I am trying to express, just with my back as I walk away, is a warning against nuclear destruction.

> *actor Kenpachiro Satsuma who wore the Godzilla suit in a 1995 Godzilla movie*

On Good All-American Advice from Miss America:

Sit by the homely girl—you'll look better by comparison.
Debra Maffett, Miss America 1982

On Good Clean Fun:

I don't think having a naked woman strapped to a rack is sexist at all. And I don't think the fact that we pretend to slit her throat is violent. It's all show biz; it's entertainment. Can't everyone understand that?

Blackie Lawless, member of rock group W.A.S.P.

On Good Questions:

I don't always wear underwear. When I'm in the heat, especially, I can't wear it. Like, if I'm wearing a flowing dress, why do I have to wear underwear?

model Naomi Campbell

On Good Reasons to Bite Off the Head of a Dead Bird:

I wanted them to remember me.
> *rocker Ozzy Osbourne on why he bit the head off a dead dove at a CBS Records meeting*

On Good Reasons to Expose Yourself:

I do expose my body, but only because I think people should have something nice to look at.
> *actress Brigitte Nielsen*

On Good Taste:

If you think it was an accident, applaud.
> *TV talk show host Geraldo Rivera to his audience on actress Natalie Wood's drowning*

On Goodbyes, Moving:

Gonna miss you bunches.
> *TV newscaster Deborah Norville saying goodbye to Jane Pauley on* The Today Show

On Grade Z Movies, Importance of:

I think *Lonely Lady* is trashy, but I think it does make a statement.
> *actress Pia Zadora promoting her movie*

On Great Achievements:

I already knew tap dancing and ballet. Now I know lap dancing, too!
> *actress Elizabeth Berkley of her role in* Showgirls

On Great People to Share a Plane Ride with:

This is it! No one will come out alive! We're all doomed!
> *talk show host Tom Snyder to other passengers onboard a turbulent plane flight*

On Groinward Directions:

I had pretty much always been promiscuous, but right after I started doing *Cheers,* well, I was going on three dates a day. As a guy, you're raised to get as much as you can. Sex, sex, sex, that's what you're after. But after a while, I realized what I was doing was foolhardy. Still, it took some time to travel from the brain . . . groinward.

actor Woody Harrelson, on his own promiscuity

On Guitars, Sensitive:

With the guitar you can have this love relationship. Without sounding too corny, you can make love to it. In relationships with women, I've found they lack understanding. The guitar understands everything. It doesn't talk back.

rocker Nuno Bettencourt, guitarist in Extreme

On Gushing, Morning News Show Hosts and:

I mean, she wore them. Sometimes to events!

Joan Lunden, then Good Morning America *host, on Princess Di's gowns that were being auctioned off*

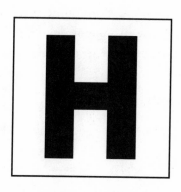

On Hamlet, Why It's Great:

I mean, it's a great story. It's got some great things in it. I mean, there's something like eight violent deaths.

actor Mel Gibson, in a school video explaining Hamlet

On Hanging, Importance of:

To get my resources, I have to hang. I have to know and be in touch with and keep the pulse of every walk of life, man.

actor Matthew McConaughey

On Happy Trails, How to Keep Them Happy:

In horse vernacular, Roy has always "given me my head," and I have tried to do the same for him.

Dale Evans, wife of Hollywood cowboy star Roy Rogers

On Heaven, Bad News and Good News about:

There aren't any real leagues here, but old teams do get together quite often to give the crowds some excitement.

> *the (supposed) ghost of baseball great Babe Ruth speaking from heaven, in an interview with* Voices from the Spirit *magazine*

On Heavy Drugs, Part One:

The worst drug today is not smack or pot, it's refined sugar. Sugar kills!

> *actor George Hamilton*

On Heavy Drugs, Part Two:

That's all I had: sugar, sugar, sugar. I was thinking of suicide. I tried to kill my brother twice! I was demented! I was psychotic! It was like a horror movie.

> *fitness guru Jack LaLanne, on his sweet tooth*

On Hebrew Winter Sports:

Among them will be the world *shalom* champion.
> *TV variety show host Ed Sullivan, announcing some winter sports champions to appear on his show*

On High School Memories, Just Your Average:

I wish I was with my friends tonight, destroying my hometown. You know, I stole seventeen cars in high school. I derailed a train with a rock. Me and my friends blew up all the thermostats in school with plastic explosives. We stole bowling balls and threw them into buildings from our cars at ninety miles an hour. We got rancid whipped cream from garbage cans at the Reddi Whip factory and put it in fire extinguishers and sprayed it on people. It was the best time of my life.
> *rocker Mark Mendoza of the Dictators*

On Historic Figures, Baseball Team Owner's Knowledge of:

Reporter: Do you think you're being Machiavellian?
George Steinbrenner: Who's he? A famous ballplayer?

> *Yankee owner George Steinbrenner during negotiations that led to former baseball commissioner Fay Vincent's banning him from baseball in 1990 (as quoted in Vincent's book proposal)*

On Holes of Fame:

These two fine gentlemen are being put in the Swimming Hole of Fame.

> *TV variety show host Ed Sullivan, introducing swimming champs Johnny Weismuller and Buster Crabbe*

On Hollywood Agents, Typical:

Super-agent Phil Gersh: I'm very sorry, but I'm drawing a blank. Do I know you?
Director Phil Aaron: I'm Phil Aaron and you're Phil Gersh, my agent.

On Hollywood, Hairsplitting and:

We won't make a sequel, but we may well make a second episode.
producer Jon Peters talking about Batman

On Hollywood Kisses, Difficult:

Could you get a little closer apart?
director Michael Curtiz to two stars in a love scene

On the Hostess with the Mostest:

This is a lovely hostess dress with a low neckline for easy entertainment.
designer Oleg Cassini on Johnny Carson's Tonight Show

On Hostesses, Slightly Overwrought:

Noooooo cooooooookies!!! No f--king cookies! I have guests who want cookies! Just what do you expect me to tell them! You f--king fool! No cookies because you didn't bother to check! And you're supposed to be in charge! You go and tell my guests that you are so stupid you forgot the cookies!

> *actress Marlo Thomas to her butler, during a luncheon she gave for Gloria Steinem, as reported in* That Girl *by Desmond Atholl*

On How to Tell if Someone's Gay, Kathleen Turner's Surefire Test of:

When I'm really hot, I can walk into a room and if a man doesn't look at me, he's probably gay.

> *actress Kathleen Turner*

On Hugh Grant, Oh-So-Self-Effacing:

I find the people there (in Hollywood) take themselves so seriously and they don't understand my self-effacing ways. I say, "Oh please, it's a terrible film and I'm awful in it," and they take me at my word. It's quite grotesque.

actor Hugh Grant

On Humanitarian Gestures, Small:

To manufacture only small sizes is a favor for humanity. I prevent ugly girls from showing off their bad figures.

designer Elio Fiorucci

On Husbands, Godlike:

I always get along fine with my women, as soon as they recognize that I am God.

producer/director John Derek

On Husbands, Helpful:

It's impossible for me to remember everybody I've made love to. . . .
I try and point them out if Rachel and I are out together and we
bump into somebody I've dated before.

> *singer Rod Stewart on his relationship with twenty-two-
> year-old wife Rachel Hunter*

On Icebreakers, Ones Not to Try:

I woke up the next morning and looked over to see this guy looking absolutely horrified and petrified.

"What's wrong," I said.

"You peed in the bed," he said.

That could well be the single most embarrassing moment of my life, even though it was a real good icebreaker for a new relationship.

actress Jenny McCarthy in her book, Jen-X

On Identity, Strong:

I'm very impressionable as far as my mom is concerned. If we're sharing something to eat, she can say, "This doesn't taste very good," and I'll be, like, "Blecch, blecch, you're right." Even if I liked it just a second before.

actress Brooke Shields

On Julio Iglesias's Son, Chip off the Old Block:

It's okay to say "girls." Women want to be called girls. You can't say, "To all the old ladies I've loved before."

singer Julio Iglesias's son, Enrique, about his father's hit song

On Inbreeding, Tasteful:

I've got taste. It's inbred in me.

actor David Hasselhoff

On Indians, Obvious Similarities of Old and New World:

Reporter: Why do you think you were invited to the White House Dinner for Indian prime minister Indira Gandhi?
Singer Wayne Newton: I'm an *American* Indian.

On Industry and Science and All Those Complicated Things, Women and:

I grew up believing that women should be nurturing and loving and let men take care of industry and science and all those complicated professions. I still believe that.

actress Teri Copley

On Information We'd Rather Not Know, Thank You:

I didn't feel well earlier. That's why I fit into this dress. I was actually in the toilet all day.

actress Jennifer Lopez, who was wearing a very tight dress at the premiere party for The Man in the Iron Mask

On Inspiration, Nauseating:

I was so used up, I said I honestly don't know if I can do it again. She said, "Let me give you my strength." She took my hands in hers and she just looked at me. We stood there with the crew working around us, and she just looked at me. I don't know what she was thinking, maybe the laundry list, but I saw in her eyes, she let me see who she was, the fears, the pain, everything . . . and I started crying. She stepped back, and we did it another time.

actress Barbara Hershey on film director Jane Campion

On Insufferability, Annoying:

I got married when Christ died. Wasn't he thirty-three when he died? We both suffered.

actor James Woods, on his divorce

On Internets, Portable:

I want an Internet. Can I have one of these?

Spice Girl Mel B. (Scary Spice) looking at a computer monitor during an America Online press conference

On Interview Questions, Great Moments in:

Liberace, are you a gentle man living in a crazy world?
> *TV host Robin Leach to Liberace on* Lifestyles of the Rich and Famous

On Interviewing Stars, Smart Questions to Ask:

Do you think I look fat in this dress?
> *comedian Janeane Garofalo at the 1996 MTV Movie Awards, in an on-air interview with Mel Gibson*

On Introductions, Enticing:

Tonight you'll be looking at some horrible scenes and meeting some horrible people.
> *TV talk show host Geraldo Rivera introducing his TV special* Murder: Live from Death Row

On Irritating Mornings with Bruce Willis:

I wake up laughing. Yes, I wake up in the morning and there I am just laughing my head off.
> *actor Bruce Willis*

On Irritation, Scalps and:

This makes me so sore it gets my dandruff up.
> *movie mogul Sam Goldwyn*

On Ivana, Great Literary Insights of:

Fiction writing is great. You can make up almost anything.
> *Ivana Trump, after writing her first novel*

On James Woods, Why Women Find Him Damn Near Irresistible:

What a looker that one is. I wonder how many guys she had to sleep with before she got her BMW.

> *actor James Woods, remarking on the driver of a passing car during a 1992 interview*

On Japanese Rock Groups, Hobbies of:

Do we have boyfriends? We are interested in delicious food and sweets. And tiny animals like the cat.

> *rocker Naoko Yamano, of Japanese rock band Shonen Knife*

On Jazz Great Thelonius Monk, MTV Knowledge of:

Who is the loneliest monk?

> *MTV news reporter Tabitha Soren after her interview with Bill Clinton in which Clinton said his dream once had been to play sax with jazz musician Thelonius Monk*

On Jenny McCarthy, Adorable Advice for Men and:

Write a love letter to a girl instead of just trying to get one to grab your pee-pee.

> *actress Jenny McCarthy in her book,* Jen-X

On Jerry Lewis, Openmindedness of, Part One:

You can't accept one individual's [opinion], particularly if it's a female and you know—God willing, I hope, for her sake it's not the case—but when they get a period, it's really difficult for them to function as normal human beings.

> *actor Jerry Lewis, responding to a harsh review from a female critic*

On Jerry Lewis, Openmindedness of, Part Two:

I was not attacking the female gender by any means—not with the type of sex drive I have, honey. I have nothing against women. As a matter of fact there's something about them I love, but I just can't put my finger on it.

actor Jerry Lewis, responding to criticism of his "normal human beings" comments

On JFK Jr., Not So Tummy-Tingling:

When I kissed [ex-boyfriend Kelly Gaines], I got a tingly feeling in my tummy that I didn't get when I kissed John Junior.

actress Brooke Shields on kissing John F. Kennedy Jr.

On Jobs, Challenging, Part One:

I don't see why anyone should put me down for my job. I'm bright. I'm intelligent. I turn letters—so what? I also talk. I talk on the show! People know my name on the show!

spokesmodel Vanna White on her role on Wheel of Fortune

On Jobs, Challenging, Part Two:

I never get bored, because there's always different puzzles, I'm wearing different clothes, there's different contestants, there's different prizes.

> *Vanna White on* Wheel of Fortune

On Jokes, Not So Hilarious:

If the men want to take off their jackets, feel free to. And, if the girls want to take off their blouses, it's all right with me.

> *media mogul Ted Turner, addressing the National Press Club*

On Julio Iglesias, Flexibility of:

I would love to have sex all the time, even in the swimming pool. I don't care if it's the deep end or shallow. I can work anyplace.

> *singer Julio Iglesias*

On Jumbo Sizes, Rambo and:

Forget about Rambo. Mark is double the size. I mean everywhere. We are dealing with a Viking here. Extra, extra, extra large.

actress Brigitte Nielsen, comparing ex Sly Stallone to lover Mark Gastineau

On Juries of One's Peers:

It was not my class of people. There was not a producer, a press agent, a director, an actor.

actress Zsa Zsa Gabor, talking about the jury that wound up convicting her of slapping a Beverly Hills police officer when he pulled her over on a traffic violation

On Just a Bunch of Nice, Responsible Guys:

We got a little place over here where we're running some whores in and out, trying to be responsible, and we're criticized for that, too.

Dallas Cowboys offensive lineman Nate Newton after a news report criticizing his activities at a house he allegedly rented

On Kate Moss, Booty of:

Kate's definitely not [white]. She's about the furthest thing from "white" there is. She's got that high-water booty. A high-water booty is important.

> *Actor Johnny Depp, explaining why dating Caucasian model Kate Moss is not the same thing as dating white women. Depp takes pride in his partial Native American background.*

On Keanu Reeves, Incredible Sensitivity of:

I cried over beauty, I cried over pain, and the other time I cried because I felt nothing. I can't help it. I'm just a cliché of myself.

> *actor Keanu Reeves*

On Kevin Costner, Romantic Views of:

If I had a choice of having a woman in my arms or shooting a bad guy on a horse, I'd take the horse. It's a lot more fun.

> *actor Kevin Costner*

On Kiddie Pop Stars, Diplomatic Abilities of:

I would like to meet Mikhail Gorbachev. I think it would be great to sit in a room with him . . . and try to make peace.

singer Donnie Wahlberg of New Kids on the Block

On Kim Basinger, Superior Comic Mind of:

Whoever wrote this doesn't understand comedy.

actress Kim Basinger, unaware that the movie she was working on was written by award-winning super-comedy writer Neil Simon

On Kim Basinger, Superior Everything Else of:

I'm a highly, highly, highly creative human being. I write music all the time. I write scripts constantly. I run my own production company. I'm also a very determined businesswoman. I've a town to deal with. I've got a lot of things to do and I don't have time to be classified as difficult, and I don't have time to care.

actress Kim Basinger

On Kirk Douglas, Enlightened Views of:

Why can't a woman be more like a dog, huh? So sweet, loving, attentive.

actor Kirk Douglas

On Language Ability, Pugilistic:

He speaks English, Spanish, and he's bilingual too.
boxing promoter Don King on boxer Julio Cesar Chavez

On Large Breasts, Unfortunate Effects of:

The wardrobe lady went into shock when I came for my fitting because my characters are supposed to have *extremely* large breasts. But she came up with these fake ones that were really cool. I loved them! I put them on and became stupid. Instantly. Not only stupid but slutty. Suddenly I was, like, checking out all the male extras.
soap actress Kelly Ripa

On the *Larry King Show*, Great Moments in:

Do you mind if I sit back a little? Because your breath is very bad.
mogul Donald Trump to Larry King while appearing on King's radio show

On Larry King's Tiny Ego:

I'm sincere. I'm really curious. I care what people think. I listen to answers and leave my ego at the door. I don't use the word "I."

talk show host Larry King to a Psychology Today *interviewer explaining why he is good at his interviewing job—and using six "I's" to do so*

On Legs, Location of:

From the waist down, Earl Campbell has the biggest legs I've ever seen on a running back.

sportscaster John Madden

On Legs, Number of:

Reporter: Which leg did Paul Warfield hurt?
Don Shula (Miami Dolphins coach): I don't know. It's one of the two.

Miami Dolphins coach Don Shula, answering questions about which leg receiver Paul Warfield hurt during practice before the upcoming Super Bowl VIII game

On Leonardo Dicaprio, Reasons for Existence:

I've been planted here to be a vessel for acting, you know what I mean?

actor Leonardo DiCaprio

On Lesbians, Televangelist Thoughts on:

I find it hard to believe, because she's so popular. She's such an attractive actress.

televangelist and politico Pat Robertson talking about Ellen DeGeneres coming out of the closet

On Life, Future of:

Life will be like a happening episode of *The Jetsons*.

singer/actress Deborah Gibson explaining what she thought the future would be like

On Life Stories, the Best Time to Write:

I don't think anybody should write his autobiography until after he's dead.

movie mogul Samuel Goldwyn

On Lifetimes, Exceeding:

I promise you this: When you lay your head down at night, if you've helped a child during that day, you've done more than you could ever do in a lifetime.

Sparky Anderson, Detroit Tiger manager

On, Like, Taxes:

Like, a lot of us are making a lot of money now, and so we're paying a lot of taxes, you know. Is there, like, a way I can just write on the memo line of my check what I want my taxes to go for, like for school?

actress Justine Bateman at a lecture given by Senator John Kerry (D-Mass.) on the Electoral College

On Linda Evangelista, Non-Mindlessness of:

People think modeling's mindless, that you just stand there and pose, but it doesn't have to be that way. I like to have a lot of input. I know how to wear a dress, whether it should be shot with me standing up or sitting. And I'm not scared to say what I think.

> *supermodel Linda Evangelista, commenting on the rigors of her chosen profession*

On Little Cody, Splitting Hairs about:

It was never my intention to "market" my son as some have cynically claimed in the press. Anyone who thinks it was "marketing" him should know about all the projects we have turned down because they were not the right sort of exposure for him.

> *TV talk show host Kathie Lee Gifford in her autobiography*

On Living, Importance of:

I think my subject matter—living—has made such an impact because it affects all of us so deeply. . . . Living is something we do take seriously.

Martha Stewart, lifestyle expert and TV personality

On Loneliness, Loneliness of:

When I get lonely, I want to be alone. I like to indulge in my loneliness so I can figure out that I'm not really lonely.

actress Alicia Silverstone

On Losing Your Virginity, Great Reasons for:

I didn't know how to wear a tampon, and I thought if I wasn't a virgin, maybe they'd fit better.

actress Valerie Bertinelli

On Love, Odor-Free:

Sometimes [they] don't smell too good, so love can have no nose.
former televangelist wife Tammy Faye Bakker, preaching
about the poor

On Loving Husbands:

I wake up every morning wishing they had killed me and Jim does, too.
Tammy Faye Bakker

On Macho, Macho Responses to:

When I see these guys write all this macho stuff I want to smash their heads.

actor John Turturro

On Macho Directors, Etiquette of:

Why are you wearing this? I can't see your breasts.

director Oliver Stone, to a female Us *magazine reporter*

On Macho Stars, Mushy:

Deep inside, I'm so . . . I mean, I'm so sensitive.

action star Jean-Claude Van Damme

On Macho Stars, the Mushiest:

I've got a talent to act. No matter what any newspaper says about me, I am one of the most sensitive human beings on earth and I know it.

action star Jean-Claude Van Damme

On Madonna as Role Model:

[I hope] my child will be a good Catholic like me.
>   *pop star Madonna*

On Madonna's Revolutionary Powers:

When Madonna grabs her crotch, the social order is effectively transgressed.
>   *professor at Florida State University who is writing a thesis called "Like a Thesis: A Postmodern Reading of Madonna Videos"*

On the Man, How to Be:

Shaq is not the man. He's the man because the NBA wants him to be the man, but before you can be the man, you've got to be the man.
>   *basketball superstar Dennis Rodman on Shaquille O'Neal*

On Marlo Thomas, Cold Cuts and:

How dare you serve cold cuts in my house. It's just so low-class and common. And white bread and pickles! And my God, *meat* lasagna!!! F--ker, you've done it again.

> *actress Marlo Thomas to her butler, as reported in* That Girl *by Desmond Atholl*

On Marriage, Fungus-Producing:

I think marriage is a custom brought about by women who then proceed to live off men and destroy them, completely enveloping the man in a destructive cocoon or eating them away like a poisonous fungus on a tree.

> *actor Richard Harris*

On Marriage, Good Reasons for:

Look at the f--ing world around us. It's an AIDS-infested world. And this woman is beautiful, talented, terrific, wanted by lots of guys. . . .

> *mogul Donald Trump, explaining why he had decided to marry Marla Maples*

On Marriage, Unappetizing:

You don't make these kinds of mistakes twice. . . . [This time] it'll be a side dish kind of thing. . . . I wouldn't want to treat it like cole slaw or anything. I guess I'd just like to think of it as spa cuisine versus a full twelve-course meal.

> *pop star Madonna explaining how she felt about marriage after her divorce from Sean Penn,* Madonna—The Book

On Marriages, Unusual:

My wife's married. I'm not.

> *basketball superstar Charles Barkley, to a female photographer*

On Marriages, Very Unusual:

We have a marriage, like a father and son.

> *boxing promoter Don King about his relationship with boxer Julio Cesar Chavez*

On Martha Stewart, Useful Things to Do with Naps and:

I catnap now and then . . . but I think while I nap, so it's not a waste of time.
> *lifestyle TV host Martha Stewart*

On Materialism, Multimillionaires and:

As a basketball fan, I get sick and tired of people talking about numbers. To me, the world is getting too materialistic.
> *basketball superstar Shaquille O'Neal after signing a seven-year $121-million contract with the Los Angeles Lakers*

On Maturer-ity:

I've always been a bit more maturer than what I am.
> *model and pop star Samantha Fox*

On Maury Povich, Importance of:

The Jewish people, for their tiny numbers, have done superbly. They don't need me. They have Einstein. They have everybody— Maury Povich.

talk show host Geraldo Rivera on the Donahue *show*

On Meetings, Real Cute:

It was so, like, *fate.*

actress Drew Barrymore on how she met Eric Erlandson (Hole guitarist) while she was throwing up outside a club

On Memories, Hard-to-Follow:

I was very hungry at a very young age. Starving. Out of my mind. Wanted to do everything I'd ever seen in the movies and more. . . . I'd just think, "What a waste of time, not being a slut!"

actress Kim Basinger

On Men, Final Word on:

I've gone for each type. . . . I don't really have a type. I have to say that men in general are a good thing.

actress Jennifer Aniston on which of her male costars is "her type"

On Men, One Woman's View:

Straight men need to be emasculated. I'm sorry. They all need to be slapped around. Women have been kept down for too long. Every straight guy should have a man's tongue in his mouth at least once.

pop star Madonna

On Men's Underwear, Crunchy:

You will enjoy a Jock Full of Nuts Special at lunchtime.

comedian Morey Amsterdam trying to say Chock Full of Nuts, one of the sponsors of his live TV show

On Metaphors, Bizarre:

It felt wonderful doing it. But that's rather like urinating in brown velvet pants. It can feel wonderful, but no one will watch.
actor Robin Williams on being in Dead Poets Society

On Metaphors, Strange Parcellian:

I'm not a bus-station kind of guy, but there are a few players here I'm not sure want to be here. They've got a brook-trout kind of look.
New England Patriots coach Bill Parcells during training camp

On Method Acting, Overdoing:

It's all very well to lie there with your eyes closed and white makeup all over your face, but to make it believable you have to believe you are dying. It was like hallucinating, I went into a place in my soul I never knew existed. I went inside a black box that I couldn't get out of, and it was like my soul and my spirit had turned into some bizarre heavy substance between coal and lead. Scary.
actress Kate Winslet on a death scene

On Mexican Movies, Problems with:

I don't like Mexican pictures. All the actors in them look too god-damn Mexican.

> *producer Jack Warner to a producer who wanted to do a film in Mexico*

On Michael Jackson, Part One:

He is the least weird man I've ever known.
> *actress Elizabeth Taylor*

On Michael Jackson, Part Two:

The biggest misconception about him is that he's weird.
> *producer Quincy Jones on Michael Jackson*

On Michael Jackson, Aerodynamics and:

We *can* fly, you know. We just don't know how to think the right thoughts and levitate ourselves off the ground.
> *singer Michael Jackson to* Newsweek *magazine*

On Mickski Jaggerski:

Jagger is rather like Dostoevsky's Brother Karamazov who, when told by his venerable brother that pain must exist so that we might learn of goodness, replied that if it was necessary that one small child should suffer in order that he should be made more aware, he did not deny the existence of God, but merely respectfully returned his ticket of admission to Heaven. That is Mick Jagger's kind of rebellion.

> *Keith Altham on Mick Jagger in* Melody Maker, *British pop magazine*

On the Midwest, Hollywood Knowledge of:

Movie mogul Sam Goldwyn to a newly signed actor: Where do you hail from?
Actor: Idaho.
Goldwyn: Out here, young man, we pronounce it Ohio.

On Minks, Mean:

Minks are mean little critters. Vicious, horrible little animals who eat their own. They're not beavers. I wouldn't wear beavers. I'd rather have a mink coat made of mean little critters that are killed in a very nice way and treated nicely for their short, mean lives so that I could keep warm.

actress Valerie Perrine

On Misconceptions, Alarming:

I'm not a psychotic bimbo cheerleader . . . people thought that for a while.

actress Jenny McCarthy

On Mistakes:

This was not a mistake. If it was a mistake, I wouldn't have done it.

NY Jets player Keyshawn Johnson, when asked if it was a mistake to say rude things about his teammates in his autobiography, Just Give Me the Damn Ball!

On Models, Big Problems with:

The big problem with dealing with older models is that they have a mind of their own.

> *Elite Model Management head John Casablancas, after he left his wife for a sixteen-year-old model*

On Models, Helpful Advice for:

Models are like baseball players. We make a lot of money quickly, but all of a sudden we're thirty years old, we don't have a college education, we're qualified for nothing, and we're used to a very nice lifestyle. The best thing is to marry a movie star.

> *supermodel Cindy Crawford*

On Models, Historical Knowledge of:

Reporter: Twiggy, do you know what happened at Hiroshima?
Twiggy: Where's that?
Reporter: In Japan . . . a hundred thousand people died on the spot.

Twiggy: Oh, God! When did you say it happened? Where? Hiroshima? But that's ghastly. A hundred thousand dead? It's frightful. Men are mad.

> *model/actress Twiggy in 1968*

On Models, Psychological Insights of:

Once I got past my anger toward my mother, I began to excel in volleyball and modeling.

> *attributed to model and pro volleyball player Gabriella Reece*

On Models, Why Few of Them are Pundits:

I would rather exercise than read a newspaper.

> *attributed to model Kim Alexis*

On Modesty, Kate Moss and:

To say this book is about me (which is the *main* reason I was uncomfortable—me, me, me, me, me . . . frightening!) is ridiculous. This book is not about me.

model Kate Moss on her book, Kate: The Kate Moss Book

On Modesty, Unspoken:

I feel like I'm the best, but you're not going to get me to say that.
San Francisco 49ers player Jerry Rice

On Moms, Strange Need to Be with Their Children and:

The notion of boarding school seems to have dipped in popularity, especially on the West Coast, where mothers and ex-wives get nutty and squeamish, wanting their little darlings around.
director Oliver Stone

On Money, the Mega-Rich and:

I'd rather not talk about money. It's kind of gross.
singer Barbra Streisand, not talking about what she was paid to direct and star in The Mirror Has Two Faces

On Morning Talk Show Hosts, Heavy Thoughts from:

I'm just amazed that I was allowed to be on TV the way I was eight years ago. I mean, I was fifty pounds heavier!
Good Morning America *host Joan Lunden*

On Morning Talk Show Hosts, Insightful Questions from:

Do you have visible wounds?
Today *host Jane Pauley to an escapee from Chinese violence*

On Most Embarrassing Moments, Michael Jackson's:

I had read Socrates, but I had never pronounced his name.
singer Michael Jackson explaining an embarrassing moment

On Movie Roles, Overidentification with:

Playing a vampire was fun. One time, someone f--ked with me on the street and I almost bit them. I realized, "Wow, man, that's a trip—I want to bite people."

actress Lili Taylor, who played a vampire in The Addiction

On Movies, Good Yet Bad:

Gregory Ratoff, film director: This is the greatest musical I have directed. It is sensational.

Jack Henley, screenwriter: Then why do you want to know whether I have time to work on the script?

Ratoff: I want you to work on it because it stinks.

On Multimillionaires, Poor:

Don Simpson had no money. Maybe $30 million at the most. That's nothing.

Ex-producer Jon Peters in Buzz Weekly. *He later told the* Daily News *he didn't say this, adding, "I'd never put Don Simpson down, he's a sweet guy."*

On Multimillionaires, Tough Moments for:

How about the guys that stand there grabbing the urinal for balance? I watch in amazement. Then they come up and say, "I'm a big fan, can I shake your hand?" And I'm a bad guy for saying, "Excuse me!" They were just holding the big wonger, and they want to shake your hand!

mogul Donald Trump

On Muscles, Reason for:

I build my body to carry my brain around.

actor Sylvester Stallone

On Name-Changes, Life-Changing Quality of:

I was very ill and afraid for my sanity but that was before I changed my name.

artist formerly known as Prince

On Native Americans, Selfish:

I don't feel we did wrong in taking this great country away from them. There were great numbers of people who needed new land, and the Indians were selfishly trying to keep it for themselves.

John Wayne, actor who played mostly cowboys in the movies

On Nauseatingly Pseudo-Philosophical Observations:

I'm old. I'm young. I'm intelligent. I'm stupid.

actor Warren Beatty

On Negotiation, Bottom Line on:

All I'm asking for is what I want.
> *baseball player Ricky Henderson on renegotiating his four-year, $12-million contract with the Oakland A's*

On New Guys in Your Life, Metaphorically Speaking:

Rod [Stewart] came into my life six weeks after I parted from Lou [Adler] and I rose back into the sky like a gull whose oil-soaked wings had been cleansed with detergent.
> *actress Britt Ekland*

On New Names, Interesting Rationale for:

My new name is Dr. Wolfgang Von Bushwickin the Barbarian Mother Funky Stay High Dollar Billstir. I call myself "Doctor" because doctors must be precise when they execute their job. The "Wolfgang" is because, on the cool, I'm into classical music, and my favorite artist is Wolfgang Amadeus Mozart. "Bushwickin" has to do with me being a father now and producing my own next of kin. So now I'm reproductive both verbally and physically. "The Barbarian" is to show that I still have the mind of a lunatic and that nothing's changed as far as me coming hardcore rough and rugged. "Mother Funky Stay High" is a manifestation of the aftermath of chronic-izm. "Dollar Bill" is because I'm currently currency in the United States and abroad. Finally, "stir" is on the end because when I kick s--t, I always manage to stir something up.

> *rapper Dr. Wolfgang Von Bushwickin the Barbarian*
> *Mother Funky Stay High Dollar Billstir, formerly known*
> *as Bushwick Bill of the Geto Boys*

On New York, Fun Visitors to:

I just love it that everyone is so rude here. It gives you the complete freedom to be rude back. If you don't like someone, you can just scream at them.

> *actress Joanne Whalley-Kilmer on New York*

On New York Mayors, a Little Too Present:

I'm here! It's me! It's Mayor Koch! I'm here!

> The People's Court *host and then-New York Mayor Ed Koch yelling to East German guards at the Berlin Wall during the Cold War*

On News Anchors, Bizarre Moments with:

Fly away, fly away, fly away home. Dan Rather reporting from New York. Thank you for joining us. Good night.

> *CBS anchor Dan Rather wrapping up his show after a report on duck hunting*

On *90210* Stars, Great Intellectual Moments of:

Howard Stern: What is the capital of New York?
Tori Spelling: . . . New Jersey?

> *Tori Spelling, actress best known for her role in* Beverly Hills 90210 *during an on-air radio interview with radio personality Howard Stern*

On Normality:

I'm just totally normal. And that's why I'm in trouble, because I'm normal and slightly arrogant. . . . A lot of people don't like themselves and I happen to be totally in love with myself. . . .
boxer Mike Tyson

On Nothing:

Nothing means nothing, but it isn't really nothing because nothing is something that isn't.
basketball star Darryl Dawkins, just before he started his vow of silence with sportswriters

On Nuclear War, Horrible Effects of:

Nuclear war would certainly set back cable.
media mogul Ted Turner

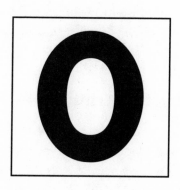

On Observations, Quantum-Mechanical:

Every minute was more exciting than the next.
> *actress Linda Evans, during an on-camera interview about the "Night of 100 Stars" party*

On Olympic Athletes, Weird:

At some point these women were all normal little girls. Somewhere along the line they got sidetracked.
> *ABC and ESPN sportscaster Al Trautwig, noting the number of women in the opening ceremonies at the Calgary Olympics*

On One-on-One Relationships, Crowded:

It's really hard to maintain a one-on-one relationship if the other person is not going to allow me to be with other people.
> *rocker Axl Rose of Guns 'n' Roses*

On Orders, Odd:

If you can't keep quiet, shut up!
film director Gregory Ratoff to his crew

On Orgasms, Expensive:

Even though the hitchhiker robs us, he gives me something that's worth the $6,000—my first orgasm. I'd pay that in a flash.
actress Geena Davis on her role in Thelma and Louise

On Oscar Acceptance Speeches, Quantum-Mechanical:

Believe me, the power and pleasure and the emotion of this moment is a constant speed of light.
Tom Hanks on getting Best Actor for Forrest Gump *in 1995*

On Oscar Acceptance Speeches, Deep Emotional Reaction to:

I was moved, man.

> *actor Steven Seagal on Tom Hanks's acceptance speech for the* Forrest Gump *Oscar*

On the Oscars, Excessive Cuteness and:

You like me! Right now! You like me!

> *actress Sally Field accepting the Oscar for* Places in the Heart *(usually misquoted as "You like me! You really like me!")*

On the Oscars, Deep Descriptions of:

It's very surreal, and then it's very, like, just a bunch of humans.

> *actress Marisa Tomei on the Oscars*

On the Oscars, Freudian Moments at:

My name is Raquel Welch. I am here for visual effects, and I have two of them.

> *Raquel Welch, appearing as a presenter for Best Visual Effects at the Academy Awards*

On the Oscars, Ultimate Word on:

The Oscars made my pits wet.

> *actor Kevin Costner*

On Ovaries, Star Ability to Produce:

I feel like the oldest ovary-producing person in America.

> *actress Susan Sarandon, mother of three children*

On Overstatements, Grandiose:

I'm everything.

> *pop star Madonna*

On Overstatements, Overactor-Style:

I don't care if people think I'm an overactor. People who think that would call Van Gogh an overpainter.

actor Jim Carrey

On Pain, Painless:

There's nothing wrong with his shoulder except some pain—and pain don't hurt you.

> *Detroit Tigers manager Sparky Anderson on a player's injury*

On Paintbrushes, Reincarnation of:

The only happy artist is a dead artist, because only then you can't change. After I die, I'll probably come back as a paintbrush.

> *actor Sylvester Stallone*

On Paris, Great Descriptions of:

Hey, like a French movie.

> *pop star Madonna, describing her first trip to Paris in* Madonna—The Book

On Parking Lots, Some Important Thoughts about:

Often we forget their beauty.
> *REM rock star Michael Stipe*

On Partial About-Faces:

I can happily say I've made a 100-degree turn in my life.
> *boxer Hector Camacho, explaining his plan to return to the ring, and presumably referring to a 180-degree turn*

On Past Lives, Bad Moments in:

I watched my head rolling on the floor. It landed face up and a big tear came out of one eye.
> *actress Shirley MacLaine describing a previous life in which she was beheaded*

On Pasta versus Proteins, Action Movie Star Comments about:

In my business, they [abdominals] are the most important muscles. That is why men can present themselves as being in shape and women cannot. Women get bloated. They cannot flush out their system of proteins. Women like to eat pasta, not proteins like fish.
actor Dolph Lundgren

On Pat Sajak, Why He Doesn't Need to Be Worried:

I just don't think America wants a female host. It's like men don't walk around in skirts in this country. Why change a good thing?
Wheel of Fortune *letter-turner Vanna White*

On Patrick Swayze, Real Smart:

There aren't many big words I don't know. But I hate people who use big words.
actor Patrick Swayze

On Patriotism, Touching:

From an early age I was aware of what America meant, and how [the Marines at Camp Pendleton] were ready to defend us at a moment's notice. I also remember what fabulous bodies those troops had.

actress Heather Locklear

On Penises, Ever-Growing:

I fall in love with all the actors in my films. They are the prolongation of my penis. Yes, my penis, like Pinocchio's nose, my penis grows!

Bernardo Bertolucci, director of such films as The Last Emperor *and* Last Tango in Paris

On Penises, *Not*-Growing:

I concentrated on my private parts trying to *will* my penis and testicles to grow. I even spoke to them. But my mind failed me. I was humiliated.

actor Marlon Brando in his autobiography Songs My Mother Taught Me

On Penises, One Woman's View:

I wouldn't want a penis. It would be like a third leg. It would seem like a contraption that would get in the way.

Madonna

On the Pentagon, Little-Known Surgical Activities of:

Prayers were offered throughout the world as Pope Paul planned for prostate surgery at the Pentagon.

newscaster Walter Cronkite, who quickly amended that to "Vatican"

On *Penthouse* Pets, Geographical Knowledge of:

Howard Stern: What country did Saddam Hussein invade during the Gulf War?
Sandi Korn, model/Penthouse Pet: Uh . . . what is . . . Jerusalem?

On *Penthouse* Pets, Good Geographical Excuses by:

I am smart, I really am. But Howard asked me about the war and I was traveling around modeling so much that I didn't keep track of things like that. I really could have sworn that we bombed Jerusalem because I have a friend in Jerusalem and I'm sure he told me Jerusalem was bombed. But Jerusalem, Iraq—it's all the same anyway.

> *Sandi Korn, model/*Penthouse *Pet/sometime girlfriend of Donald Trump, explaining herself in Howard Stern's* Private Parts

On People and Golf Courses, Odd Similarity of:

Reporter, asking about famous golfer Tiger Woods: What do you think of Tiger Woods?
Sandy Lyle, pro golfer: I don't know. I've never played there.

On Perfect Moms:

Kathie Lee Gifford to her son Cody: I won't talk about you on the show, if it's not okay with you. But then Mommy's going to have to find a new job, and you might not be able to go to Disneyland anymore.

> *Gifford as quoted in The* "I Hate Kathie Lee Gifford" *Book*

On Perfect Women, an Actor's View:

The patience of a saint, spunk, and a head flat enough to set a can of beer on.

> *actor Robert Hays describing his perfect woman*

On Perfection:

If only I had a little humility, I'd be perfect.

> *cable TV mogul Ted Turner*

On Personal Questions:

Ask us about our cup size or our favorite position, but—please—no personal questions.

> *model Sharon Barbi (who appeared with her twin sister Shane on a* Playboy *cover) when asked which sister was older*

On Pete Townshend, Potential Problems Checking Box "M" or "F"

I know how it feels to be a woman because I am a woman. And I won't be classified as just a man.

> *rock star Pete Townshend on his sexuality*

On Photographers, Tough Life of:

I felt so sorry for him. I thought, "This poor man is going through all of this for just half a nipple."

> *singer La Toya Jackson about the* Playboy *photographer who shot her pictures*

On Physicians, Ones to Avoid:

I don't know what kind of doctor I am. But watching all these beautiful sisters here . . . I'm debating whether I should be a gynecologist.

> *boxer Mike Tyson, on being given honorary degree from*
> *Central State University in Wilberforce, Ohio*

On Pi, Snappy Definitions of:

Reporter: Do you remember what "pi" is?
Actress Nicolette Sheridan: Pi is pi.

On Pick-Ups, Great Moments in:

We met on New Year's Eve 1994. . . . He came up, grabbed me, and licked my face. I thought he was a nice guy and gave him my phone number.

> *actress Pamela Anderson Lee, in* Pandemonium, *talking*
> *about meeting her future husband, Tommy Lee*

On Political Correctness, Coaches and:

I told him to take a picture of his testicles so he'd have something to remember them by if he ever took another shot like the last one. For you ladies, that's t-e-s-t-i-c-l-e-s.

> *Indiana University basketball coach Bobby Knight, 1990, when asked about heated exchange with one of his players*

On Politically Correct Questions, Aging Rock Stars and:

What do women need money for?
> *rock star Mick Jagger*

On Poop, Pop:

We're human. We doo-doo in the toilets and do everything people do.
> *pop star Jonathan Knight of the New Kids on the Block talking about the band*

On Posing Nude for Playboy, God and:

I thought, "This is great. . . . Something good that God created. This is how a woman should be seen."

> *model and personality Jessica Hahn on posing nude for* Playboy

On Predictions, Bad:

I'd rather be dead than singing "Satisfaction" when I'm forty-five.

> *rock star Mick Jagger before he hit forty-five—and who is* still *performing "Satisfaction"*

On Predictions, Not So Good:

I'm going to be bigger than the Beatles.

> *Irish singer Crispian St. Peters after his 1966 hit "You Were on My Mind"*

On Predictions, Tough:

Predictions are difficult, especially about the future.
>*baseball great Yogi Berra*

On Predictions, We've Heard Better:

That's a face you'll never see on a lunchbox.
>*NBC chief Brandon Tartikoff talking about Michael J. Fox—who had just been cast in* Family Ties, *the TV show that made him a star*

On Predivorce Dialogue, Great Moments in:

Marla Maples: Are you in love with your husband? Because I am.
Ivana Trump: Stay away from my husband.
Marla: I love him, and if you don't, why don't you let him go?
Ivana: You stay away from my husband, or else.
Donald: You're overreacting.
>*heated conversation on the ski slopes between Donald Trump, his then-wife Ivana, and his then-girlfriend Marla, as reported by* Time *magazine*

On Prenuptial Agreements, Bad Predictions about:

I would never sign a prenuptial agreement, that makes the relationship so shallow.

Marla Maples, before her marriage to Donald Trump

On Presence, Continuity of:

I'm impressed by the continuity of his physical presence.

sportscaster Howard Cosell commenting on a quarterback

On Preventing World War II, Yoko Ono's Theories of:

If I was a Jewish girl in Hitler's day, I would become his girlfriend. After ten days in bed, he would come to my way of thinking.

Yoko Ono on how she would have stopped Hitler

On the President, Mr. G.'s Views on:

I mean, I'm a guy from Brooklyn and, you know, you shake hands with the President and take a picture. It's like, "Mr. G., the President. Mr. President, Mr. G." It was a bunch of weathermen from fifty of the top markets and after I shook the President's hand, the first thing he said to me was, "What's happening?" I guess that's the kind of guy he is. . . .

New York City TV weatherman Mr. G. on meeting President Clinton

On Princess Lay-a, Metaphorically Speaking

The meaning of the title is pornographic, but I'm using it metaphorically.

actress/writer Carrie Fisher on her novel Surrender the Pink

On Promises, Disappointing:

That's the last time I'm going to cook in the nude.

cable talk show host Robin Byrd after accidentally burning her breasts on a baking pan

On Proof, Indisputable:

Women are here to serve men. Look at them, they got to squat to piss. Hell, that proves it.

Hustler *founder Larry Flynt*

On Psychiatric Contributions by Aaron Spelling, Great:

Do you know what our suicide rate would be if we didn't have television? Do you know how much happiness I've brought to people who couldn't get out of the house but could watch *Love Boat*?

Aaron Spelling, producer of TV hits like Beverly Hills 90210 *and* Melrose Place

On Putting the Spice Back into Your Marriage, Garth Brooks's Friendly Hints and:

I'm not telling anybody, "If you're not happy, go out and screw around because your wife will become a dynamo for you." But I got to be honest with you—that's what happened for me.

singer Garth Brooks discussing marriage

On Questions, Answerable:

Ingrid! Ingrid! Whatever got into you?
> *Louella Parsons, legendary Hollywood gossip columnist, on the radio after news came that actress Ingrid Bergman was pregnant out of wedlock*

On Questions, Odd:

What would happen if you melted? You know, you never really hear this talked about that much, but spontaneous combustion? It exists! . . . [People] burn from within. . . . Sometimes they'll be in a wooden chair and the chair won't burn, but there'll be nothing left of the person. Except sometimes the teeth. Or the heart. No one speaks about this—but it's for real.
> *actor Keanu Reeves*

On Questions, Interesting:

Do you want to pet my pussy?
> *Actress Raquel Welch, carrying her pet cat, to talk show host Johnny Carson. (This is also attributed to Zsa Zsa Gabor during a* Tonight Show *appearance.)*

On Questions Little Puppy Tuppins Couldn't Answer:

As I lay on the floor in my dark, empty room, Tuppins, my puppy, licked at the tears running down my face. "Oh, Tuppins," I sobbed. "Why has God forsaken me?"
> *Tammy Faye Bakker, former televangelist and wife of convicted televangelist Jim Bakker, on the last night she spent in her house before being evicted by Jerry Falwell in 1988*

On Questions to Think about:

I never watched anybody make love, so how do you know if you're doing it right?
actor Kevin Costner

On Questions, Unanswerable:

After reading this book, the first thing I thought was if art imitates life, then where have I been *not* being Isaac Mizrahi all these years?
John F. Kennedy Jr., on a jacket blurb for designer Isaac Mizrahi's book The Adventures of Sandee the Supermodel

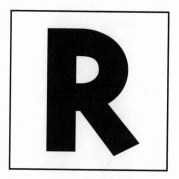

On Rape, the Snuggly Kind:

It's not going to be a violent rape, where the guy rapes her and kills her. It's going to be a friendly rape.
>   *actor Michael Paré about a TV show dealing with date rape*

On Rappers, Philanthropic:

Usually they send pictures, some of them tempting. But I get some ugly ones, too. I give those to the home boys.
>   *rapper Ton-Loc about the photos female fans send him*

On Real Cool, Jiggy Cool:

Gettin' jiggy wit it is, like, the next level of cool. It's cool to the eighth power. Some people are fly, some people are kind of hot. But when you are the jiggiest, when you exude jiggy-essence, it's the acme of cool.
>   *actor/rapper Will Smith, explaining the title of his hit "Gettin' Jiggy Wit It"*

On Real-Life Aliens, Scientific-Actress Thoughts about:

They vibrate on another energy level than we do.

> X-Files *star Gillian Anderson, describing why real-life aliens, which she believes are on the planet, are frightening to Earth people. (She also added that she believes the government knows about these aliens, but is covering it up.)*

On Real Life, Young Multimillionaire's Knowledge of:

My father wrote hippie music and my sister wrote cheesy '80s music. I'm writing about what's real. I'm writing about giving crack to the inner cities.

> *model Bijou Phillips*

On the *Real* Reason Mick Isn't Prime Minister:

I'm thinking about entering politics—I'd love to do it. But I haven't got the right wife.

> *rock star Mick Jagger*

On Reasons for Hiring a Ghostwriter to Write Your Autobiography, Good:

I don't know all the certain words to word it.

> *rapper Vanilla Ice on why his autobiography had a ghost writer*

On Reasons for Importing Entire Castles from Abroad, Good:

I don't like stucco.

> *actor Nicholas Cage, explaining why he's bringing a castle over from England "stone by stone" for himself and wife Patricia Arquette to live in*

On Reasons Why More Race Car Drivers Aren't Winning Elections for Governor:

If I was the governor of any state, I'd have the death penalty for litterbugs.

> *racing car great Mario Andretti*

On Redundance, Redundant:

Let us reflect back nostalgically on the past.
sportscaster Howard Cosell

On Relationships, Planetary:

It's what you call Plutonic.
boxing promoter Don King explaining his relationship with Mike Tyson's then-wife Robin Givens

On Religious Holidays, Bad Scheduling of:

You mean they've scheduled Yom Kippur opposite *Charlie's Angels?*
noted TV programmer Fred Silverman, when told that Yom Kippur fell on a Wednesday

On Religious Symbols, Interesting Aspects of:

Crucifixes are sexy because they've got a naked man on the front.
pop star Madonna, who also apparently doesn't realize that Christ wears a loincloth

On Rock Stars, Articulateness of:

I always think it's cool to commemorate cool things that have happened, because there's a chance that you may, through commemorating them, evoke them again.

Spin Doctors's Chris Barron at Woodstock II

On Rock Stars, Intellectual Titans:

Overall, the unpredictable nature of the combined images in the poster produce a sense of unease. For me, the poster (advertising the Montreux Jazz Festival) suggests both the festivity of the event itself but also resurrects the spectre of an unwilling alliance we have made with destructive forces. As in any social confrontation, it contains contradictory information. It is not presented as the pairing of dichotomies but rather, as a full spectrum. It can be seen as a merging of cultural conditions rather than their polarization.

David Bowie, rock star, writing about something or other in Crankin' Out: the David Bowie magazine

On Rock Stars, Out of This World:

At first the press said I was a gimmick, but how can I be? I'm a real person. I was born on Mars many aeons ago. I was around when dinosaurs were around. I've always had dreams of T. rex chasing me, and he got me. Since then, I've lived many different lives. When I return in another life form I may be a tennis player or a basketball player because I'm very athletic.

lead singer ? of ? and the Mysterians

On Rock Stars, Starving:

Jerry died broke. We only have a few hundred thousand dollars in the bank.

Deborah Koons Garcia, wife of Grateful Dead's Jerry Garcia.

On Rock Stars, Well-Bred:

I'm not a snob. Ask anybody. Well, anybody who matters.

rock star Simon LeBon of Duran Duran

On Rock, Ultimate Mission of:

I believe rock can do anything: it's the ultimate vehicle for everything. It's the ultimate vehicle for saying anything, for putting down anything, for building up anything, for killing and creating. It's the absolute ultimate vehicle for self-destruction, which is the most incredible thing, because there's nothing as effective as that—not in terms of art, anyway, or what we call art. You just can't be as effectively self-destructive if you're a writer, for example, or a painter; you just can't make sure that you're never going to f--king raise your head again. Whereas if you're a rock star you really can.

rock star Peter Townshend of The Who

On Rocks, Girlish:

My best friend is a rock. They've very inspirational. . . . Every color, every texture [in my menswear collection] has been inspired by sitting on this rock. It's wonderful for menswear, but I find rocks very female.

fashion designer Donna Karan

On Role Models, Marla Maples and:

I'm so excited to meet you. I've always modeled myself after Ginger.
> *starlet Marla Maples, then Donald Trump's girlfriend, when meeting actress Tina Louise—"Ginger" on* Gilligan's Island

On the Rolling Stones, Like:

Are they, like, old?
> *Spice Girl fan, when asked if she knew who the Rolling Stones were*

On Rolls-Royces, the Big Problem with:

You just cannot drive a Rolls-Royce in Beverly Hills anymore because they have it in for you.
> *actress Zsa Zsa Gabor*

On the Roman Empire:

It's like the Roman Empire. Wasn't everybody running around just covered with syphilis? And then it was destroyed by the volcano.
actress Joan Collins

On Romance, Fiscal:

I need someone I have verbal and spiritual collateral with, where I can go to the bank and withdraw some of her feelings and knowledge.
actor Sylvester Stallone

On Salaries, Minor:

It's not a million-dollar-a-year contract. We're talking about a really large sum of money.

> *basketball star Larry Bird*

On Samaritans, Very Friendly:

It's not the first hooker that I've helped out. I was being a Good Samaritan.

> *actor Eddie Murphy after being caught picking up a transvestite in West Hollywood at 4:45 A.M.*

On Same Normal Lives, Models and:

It's just my same normal life, but now I get to go to movie premieres and to parties.

> *model Bridget Hall*

On Satisfaction:

I should think that being my old lady would be all the satisfaction or career any woman needs.

rock star Mick Jagger

On Sexual Harassment, Vanna's Fascinating Insights on:

Guys make passes at me and blow whistles at me. I just throw it off my back. I don't think anything of it. That's the way it is. If someone raped me, that's a different story.

Vanna White, talking about why charges against Supreme Court Justice nominee Clarence Thomas were "blown way out of proportion"

On Schmuck, Donald Trump not a:

I'm not a schmuck. Even if the world goes to hell in a handbasket, I won't lose a penny.

mogul Donald Trump

On Self-Assessment, Painfully Honest:

One thing's for sure: now when I look at *Funny Girl,* I think I was gorgeous. I was too beautiful to play Fanny Brice.
actress Barbra Streisand

On Self-Image, Too Much:

I'm wicked. I'm sexy. I'm heaven.
actor Matthew McConaughey during a photo shoot

On Self-Images, Unique:

I am not a demon. I am a lizard, a shark, a heat-seeking panther. I want to be Bob Denver on acid playing the accordion.
actor Nicholas Cage

On Self-Loathing, Reasons for:

Good-looking people turn me off. Myself included.
actor Patrick Swayze

On Sequels:

I will never do *Pulp [Fiction] 2* but having said that, I could very well do other movies with these characters.
> *director Quentin Tarantino*

On Sex, Problems with:

After you hit a home run you get to be with the guys, and after sex, well, you know. . . .
> *actor D. B. Sweeney on which he liked better, home runs or sex*

On Sex Symbols, Philosophers and:

Reporter: Do you read Kierkegaard?
Pamela Anderson Lee: Uh, what movies was he in?
> *conversation between film reporter and actress Pamela Anderson Lee while she was promoting her film* Barb Wire, *and obviously unaware that Kierkegaard is a famous existential philospoher*

On Shakespeare:

I think that Shakespeare is a s--t. Absolute s--t! He may have been a genius for his time, but I just can't relate to that stuff. "Thee and thous"—the guy sounds like a faggot.

rocker Gene Simmons of Kiss

On Shakespeare, Condensed Version

Reporter: Did you read the original Shakespearean version of *Othello*?

Actor Lawrence Fishburne (who was acting in a contemporary version of *Othello* in which two-thirds of the dialog was cut): Why should I read all those words that I'm not going to get to say?

On Shakespeare, Hollywood Producer Knowledge of:

Actor Edward G. Robinson: Sam, my studio is going to make *The Merchant of Venice*. They want me to play Shylock. Should I accept?

Movie mogul Sam Goldwyn: Screw 'em. Tell 'em you'll only play the Merchant.

On Shakespeare, Modern Interpretations of:

Juliet's so happy and in love, but at the same time so sad and lonely. She's totally neurotic. I could really relate.

> *actress Alicia Silverstone in an interview about her movie role as Juliet in* Romeo and Juliet

On Shaquille O'Neal, Just a Regular Guy . . . :

Everything is just money, money, money. All I want to do is play basketball, drink Pepsi, and wear Reebok.

> *basketball star Shaquille O'Neal on his new multimillion dollar contract*

On Sharon Stone's Ego, Not-So-Small, Part One:

Any man in Hollywood will meet me if I want that. No, make that any man *anywhere*.

> *actress Sharon Stone*

On Sharon Stone's Ego, Not-So-Small, Part Two:

If I was just normally intelligent, I could probably get away with it—but I'm *fiercely* intelligent and that's threatening.
actress Sharon Stone

On Shows about Underpants, Eternal Popularity of:

I have a show that's basically about underpants, and everybody sort of wears them and likes them, and I know all you people do, and that's why you voted for us.
actress Kirstie Alley, after winning a People's Choice Award for her TV show Veronica's Closet

On Similarities, Similar:

They're very much alike in a lot of similarities.
baseball manager Casey Stengel, comparing New York Yankees second baseman Billy Martin to Chicago White Sox second baseman Nellie Fox

On Similes, Clever Rock:

I like to think of us as Clearasil on the face of the nation. Jim Morrison would have said that if he was smart, but he's dead.
avant-rocker Lou Reed on his band

On the Simple Life, Barbra Streisand and:

I want only two houses, rather than seven. . . . I feel like letting go of things.
singer Barbra Streisand

On Single Women, Garbage-Y:

Reporter: Do you think you'll get married again?
Ivana Trump: Absolutely. I am not garbage—a single-girl type.

On Singularity:

David Cone is in a class by himself with three or four other players.
New York Yankees owner George Steinbrenner, about his ace pitcher

On Slips, Freudian:

They've [the Clinton administration] grown so accustomed to their own demagoguery . . . that even when confronted with the truth they still apparently, without any conscience, look into the camera just as I am now, and continue to lie about it.

conservative talk show host Rush Limbaugh

On Smashing Up Hotel Rooms, Logical Reasons for:

Smoke can drive me mad. Otherwise, it's not getting things you've paid for. That's why we used to smash up hotels—not because we had nothing better to do, but because you're paying top money and you weren't getting any respect.

singer Rod Stewart

On Soap Opera Line Readings, Freudian:

Doc, we've got a lot to consider here. And I'm not just talking about my vows, I'm taking about what's besth—beh—wha—what breasts . . .

> *soap opera star Drake Hogestyn blowing a line during a* Days of Our Lives *taping*

On Space, Insightful Views of:

I think space exploration is very important. I think there is very intelligent life on Mars. I believe that Martians are spying on us from the bottom of the ocean.

> *actress Annabella Sciorra on her part in the NBC sci-fi miniseries* Astronome

On Spaceflight, Interesting Ideas about:

One time I imagined myself as a giant penis launching off from Earth like a spaceship. I think the whole space program is based on a deep psychological recognition that this world is ending and that we had better conquer new worlds soon.

actor Cary Grant

On Spelling, Baseball and:

Right now, I have the three C's: comfortable, confident, and seeing the ball well.

Mariner outfielder Jay Buhner

On Sports Stars, Success Secrets of:

I strive on pressure.

basketball star Magic Johnson

On Squid, Macho:

A squid, as you know of course, has ten testicles.
television chef Graham Kerr

On Staircases, Legal:

I don't want to get into that, but Mike's got a whole new set of banisters.

boxing promoter Don King when asked if Mike Tyson was getting new lawyers

On Steven Spielberg, Too Busy for Minor Annoyances Like Reading:

I wouldn't have filmed *The Color Purple* if the book had been a big fat novel. The reason I read it is because it is thin.
director Steven Spielberg

On Sting, Why He Looks Frustrated:

The purpose of sex ideally is for the woman to attain orgasm and for the man not to.

rock star Sting in a Rolling Stone *interview*

On Strip Clubs, What They Really Are:

It's about time that people forget that image of strip clubs as seedy places. . . . Rather, today's strip clubs are capital-intensive female-empowerment zones. . . .

actress Demi Moore

On Supermodels, Camaraderie and:

I think it makes women feel better to find fault with other women. I do that, too.

supermodel Tyra Banks

On Supermodels, Diverse Abilities of:

I can do anything you want me to do as long as I don't have to speak.

> *supermodel Linda Evangelista (who once bragged that she wouldn't wake up for less than $10,000)*

On Supermodels, Existential:

Elevator passenger: Where do you want to go?
Model Claudia Schiffer: I don't know. I've never been there.

> *conversation when Schiffer walked into the occupied elevator, hit a button that didn't light up because the floor was unoccupied, then continued to hold down the button*

On Supermodels, Horrible Truth about:

Richard doesn't really like me to kill bugs, but sometimes I can't help it.

> *supermodel Cindy Crawford commenting on her then-husband Richard Gere and his beliefs as a Buddhist*

On Supermodels, Such Fascinating People . . . :

I haven't seen the Eiffel Tower, Notre Dame, the Louvre. I haven't seen anything. I don't really care.

supermodel Tyra Banks

On Super-Skinny Supermodels, Self-Discipline of:

It was kind of boring for me to have to eat. I would know that I had to, and I would.

supermodel Kate Moss, known for her "waif" look

On Superstars, Importance of Hair for:

I looked at all the superstars. What is their different thing? Their hair . . . I wanted to be a star. I said, "I have to fix my hair."

Rob Pilatus, one-half of Grammy-winning group Milli Vanilli who were later found to be lip-synching to prerecorded songs sung by other singers, commenting on his over $700 hairstyle

On Sylvester Stallone's Film *Assassins*, Surprising Intellectuality of:

[It's an] existential action film. . . . Screenplay by Sartre. Dialogue by Camus.

actor Sylvester Stallone

On Symbols of Success:

I'm much more than a pair of breasts. . . . I represent success, hard work, and fun.

actress Pamela Anderson Lee

On Tabloid TV Show Goals, Impressive:

If we're going to do the Playmate stories, let's make them a little more intellectual.

> Inside Edition *anchor Deborah Norville, in a* Chicago Tribune *article about doing stories she called "the centerfold stuff"*

On Taking Charge of Your Life Before It Happens:

I have the distinct feeling that I chose my family. . . . In the next [lifetime] I may be even more causative.

> *actor John Travolta on his previous lives*

On Talk Show Hosts, Non-PC Jokes by:

I like the women's movement—from behind.

> *conservative talk show host Rush Limbaugh*

On Talk Shows, Great Moments in:

It is very difficult to come on and describe your private parts.
> *talk show host Sally Jessy Raphael thanking guests who had appeared on her "Sexual Confusion" hour*

On Talk Shows, Great Moments in:

Okay, our focus: Are Babies Being Bred for Satanic Sacrifice? Controversial to say the least. Unbelievable to say the least. Disgusting to say the least. We'll be right back.
> *talk show host Geraldo Rivera, introducing a commercial break on his show*

On Talk Show Hosts, Exciting Physical Characteristics of:

It used to be that you couldn't touch some girls with a ten-foot pole. Well, I was the guy with the twelve-foot pole.
> *talk show host Mike Douglas, during an interview with actress Dyan Cannon*

On Talk Show Hosts, Job Perks of:

You know, Jack, I go to sleep with you every night.
>*actress Eva Gabor, trying to tell* Tonight Show *host Jack Paar that she watched his late show every night*

On Talk Show Hosts, Kissing and Telling and . . . :

I rowed us to a secluded spot. . . . Right there the estranged First Lady of Canada lent new meaning to the term "head of state."
>*talk show host Geraldo Rivera on his alleged affair with Margaret Trudeau, then the Canadian Prime Minister's wife*

On Talk Show Hosts, Probing:

Raquel, before I get into you, I must pause for this commercial.
>*talk show host David Frost to guest Raquel Welch*

On Talk Shows, Tasteful Moments on, Part One:

We are told, Tommy, and this may come as a surprise to you, that you have a thirteen-year-old son who is watching this program right now, who has just been told that you are his father and that you are a murderer.

> *talk show host Geraldo Rivera to death row inmate Tommy Arthur, in prison in Alabama for killing his wife's sister*

On Talk Shows, Tasteful Moments on, Part Two:

Your wife wants you to die. Your reaction, quickly.
> *Geraldo Rivera to Tommy Arthur*

On Talk Shows, X-Rated Animal Segments on:

Stay tuned, because right after this we're going to be seeing a horny owl.

> *talk show host Johnny Carson, introducing an animal trainer with a horned owl*

On Taste, Exquisite:

I want to play in a movie with a lot of frontal nudity and sex scenes. When I see a movie, I rate it on how many times I see people undressed. *Henry and June* gets fifty-five stars; *GoodFellas* none.

Paul Hipp, star of Buddy: The Buddy Holly Story *on Broadway*

On Tattoos, Amazing Symbolic Importance of:

Tattoos are like stories. They're symbolic of the important moments in your life. Sitting down, talking about where you got each tattoo and what it symbolizes is really beautiful. Body piercing, too, I think is beautiful.

actress Pamela Anderson Lee, who refused to say where she is pierced

On Team Owners, Sensitive and Caring:

I feel cheated.

> *Cincinnati Reds owner Marge Schott, when the opening day ball game was canceled after the death of umpire John McSherry*

On Temples of Learning, Deep:

I like my pussy. Sometimes I stare at it in the mirror when I'm undressing. I love my pussy. It is the complete summation of my life. . . . My pussy is the temple of learning.

> *pop star Madonna*

On Terms of Endearment:

In my young days, I used to pick up sluts, and I don't mean that nastily. It's more a term of endearment, really, for girls who know how to speak their minds.

> *actor Kevin Costner*

On Telethons, Importance to World Order and:

Why am I a criminal? What we are doing here is great work. . . . We've only been at peace 557 days in the last seventeen thousand years. Had they had telethons, we'd have had peace, I'm sure. Is that idealistic? Is that old-fashioned, mid-Victorian? Is that stupid? Is that rhetoric? No! That's what I believe.

> *actor/telethon host Jerry Lewis responding to critics who questioned his motives for doing telethons*

On Television, Quality:

. . . Drinking blood . . . grave robbing . . . mutilated animals . . . drinking her fifteen-year-old victim's blood . . . gouged out his victim's eyes . . . butchered his mother . . . cut the ears off . . . drinking his own blood . . . The acts . . . are so horrible that the question could fairly be raised again: Why are we doing this broadcast?

> *talk show host Geraldo Rivera on his NBC special*
> Devil Worship: Exposing Satan's Underground

On Television Scheduling, Peculiar:

Just remember, folks, next Monday night *Password* will be seen on Thursday evening.

> Password *game show host Allen Ludden*

On Temporary Permanence:

It could permanently hurt a batter for a long time.

> *baseball star Pete Rose, speaking about a brushback pitch*

On Tennis, Touching Moments in:

Newscaster: Tell me, now that your husband is a tennis professional, do you watch him play?
Model Jinx Falkenburg: Too nervous. But just before a match I always kiss his balls.

On Test Scores, Modest Actor's Specificity about:

Yeah, I scored eight hundred on the verbal part of the SATs and 779 on the math. Why does everybody talk about this? Who gives a s--t?

> *actor James Woods, quoted in the September 1989 issue of* Smart *magazine*

On Test Scores, More From a Modest Actor Than We Want to Know about:

I was a straight A student in high school and I never did anything but show up. . . . I took the Stanford-Binet IQ test, and I guess 180 is the highest it will go, and I got them all right. I didn't miss one. My score was 180 plus.

> *actor James Woods*

On Things to Remember to Tell the Kids, Important:

No one had ever told me about prostitution—that it was immoral or illegal.

> Father Knows Best *actress Lauren "Kitten" Chapin who turned tricks to support her drug habit*

On Things We'd Rather Not Hear about:

When I got through with the twin pregnancy, my abdominal skin was such that I had to fold it up and then stick it in my pants.
actress Cybill Shepherd

On Thoughts, Charitable:

Whenever I . . . turn on TV [I] am reminded of the millions of women who have stringy hair, large pores, overweight figures, and rough hands.

actor Warren Beatty

On Thoughts, Skin-Deep:

I don't think I was born beautiful. I just think I was born me.
model Naomi Campbell

On Throats, Crowded:

Everyone wants to jump into my throat!
Michael Curtiz, Hollywood director, complaining to his assistant

On Tips of the Slongue:

Milton, we owe you a gret of dadditude.
talk show host Mike Douglas, known for his spoonerisms, to Milton Berle

On Titanic Actresses, Impressionable:

She [Emma Thompson] opened the door and she said, "Hi, you must be Kate, I'm Emma. I've just gotta go for a wee, I'll see you in a minute," and I thought, "I love her."

actress Kate Winslet, Emma Thompson's costar in Sense and Sensibility

On Tolerance, Brigitte Bardot and:

If tomorrow Muslims stop slitting sheep's throats, I will find them the most wonderful people in the world. I am not racist if one behaves normally.

French star Brigitte Bardot, apparently unaware that several billion non-Muslims also kill animals for food

On Tough Jobs, Really Grueling:

It's not as easy as it looks, being on all the time. I mean, what happens if I'm in a bad mood?

Wheel of Fortune *costar Vanna White*

On Tough Times in TV Land:

I'm down. I'm scared. I don't know what the answers are. Hold me.
> *actor Paul Michael Glaser, star of TV cop show* Starsky
> and Hutch, *to his costar David Soul on the* Starsky and
> Hutch *set when things weren't going well*

On Trailblazing, Geraldo Rivera and:

That's what happens when you're ahead of your time. When I die, people will understand.
> *talk show host Geraldo Rivera on being fired from
> ABC in 1985*

On True Confessions, Annoying:

As a teenager, I crept around on eggshells because people kept telling me I could destroy men.
> *actress Cybill Shepherd*

On True Confessions, More Annoying:

I was Miss Congeniality in the Miss Teenage America Pageant. I don't tell that to many people—I've always felt that was so embarrassing. But really—that's really who I am. That's me.

actress Cybill Shepherd

On True Happiness, Nauseating:

Making love in the morning got me through morning sickness—I found I could be happy and throw up at the same time.

actress Pamela Anderson Lee

On True Love:

Even if she weren't an actress, it would still be very important to have her [Brooke Shields] in my life.

tennis star Andre Agassi on his wife, actress Brooke Shields

On True Success:

I didn't know I could top *Knight Rider*.
> *attributed to David Hasselhoff, star of* Baywatch, *which is seen in 140 different countries by over one billion people*

On Truisms, True:

I've got my faults, but living in the past isn't one of them. There's no future in it.
> *Detroit Tigers manager Sparky Anderson*

On Trump Tower versus the Empire State Building, the World Trade Center, the Taj Mahal, the White House, the Capitol Building . . . :

There has never been anything like this built in four hundred years.
> *mogul Donald Trump on his Trump Tower penthouse*

On Trump versus World Leaders, Statesmen, Nobel Prize Winners, Scientists, Religious Leaders, Doctors Born in the Same Year

There's no one my age who has accomplished more. Everyone can't be the best.

mogul Donald Trump on himself

On Trying Again . . . and Again . . . and Again . . . and . . . :

If I don't make this one last, there's something wrong with me.
actor Mickey Rooney, on marriage number three, 1949
This one is for keeps. We're really in love.
Mickey Rooney, marriage number four, 1952
The perfect end to an imperfect journey.
Mickey Rooney, marriage number five, 1959
It's unimportant how many times a person is married. We don't think in chronological numbers. Margie's my wife and we're sure this is a good one.
Mickey Rooney, marriage number six, 1966

I am my own man for the first time.

Mickey Rooney, during marriage number seven

At last I've found the real one.

Mickey Rooney, marriage number eight, 1975

His previous wives just didn't understand him.

Twenty-five-year-old Jan Chamberlain, Mrs. Mickey
Rooney number eight

On TV Remotes, Good Reasons for Inventing:

If you're sitting around after a show and there's something you don't
like, you just switch it off by throwing a bottle through the screen.

rock drummer Keith Moon

On Twenty-Dollar Bills, Top-Secret Facts
Revealed about:

This [the threads in a twenty-dollar bill] is so the United States gov-
ernment can scan you. They [the U.S. government] can tell if you're
carrying too much currency. When I showed this to my husband,

it really wowed him. When I pulled out this little spy trick, he knew how well he'd done with me.

> *actress Patricia Arquette (and wife of actor Nicolas Cage), during an* Us *magazine interview—in which she pulled out a twenty-dollar bill, ripped off a corner and pointed out the threads in the bill to the reporter*

On Twenty-Five-Year-Old Twenty-Three-Year-Olds:

He's [Johnny Bench] the best twenty-three-year-old catcher I've seen since Campy [Roy Campanella]—and Campy was twenty-five years old the first time I saw him.

> *baseball manager Casey Stengel*

On the Two-Party System, One Model's Take:

Howard Stern: What political party is President Bush a member of?
Sandi Korn (model/Penthouse Pet): I know he's either a Republican or the other one . . . but I don't know. I would say Democrat.

On Two-Way Descriptions:

I only know how to play two ways and that's reckless and abandon.
basketball star Magic Johnson

On Ugly Sports Jackets, Trauma of:

In the end I said, "What's the matter? Is it the coat?" and I started to cry. . . . That was probably the worst day of my life, except for when my father died.

actor John Malkovich recalling a "kind of traumatic thing" that occurred when he was wearing a sports jacket that no one liked while appearing in the play Burn This *in New York*

On Ultraviolent Films, Obvious Lighthearted Reasons to Make:

I did it [made *Natural Born Killers*] out of a sense of fun and irreverence.

director Oliver Stone, explaining why he wrote and directed Natural Born Killers—*a film about two mass murderers lionized by the media. . . . and one that allegedly inspired a seventeen-year-old boy to kill his stepmother and half-sister in Utah*

On Understatements:

It weren't clever.

> *rocker Ozzy Osbourne after he bit off the head of a dead bat at an Iowa concert and had to get a series of painful rabies shots*

On Upbringing, Tough:

People have this impression that we came from an upper-class upbringing because we had a Citroën and three kids went to a private school.

> *director Spike Lee's sister, Joie Lee, answering accusations that her brother isn't the tough street-smart person he pretends to be*

On Ups and Downs:

I am not going to sit here and stand for those kind of insults

> *conservative talk show host Rush Limbaugh*

On Validity, Plasticity and:

I wanted my anger to be valid, and the only way to do that is to be fairly attractive.

> *singer Courtney Love on why she had bleached-blond hair, a nose job, and is always on a diet*

On Very Bad Excuses, Johnny Depp and, Part One:

There was a bug in the place that I was trying to kill. This thing had tried to attack me and tried to suck my blood—a big cockroach. And I tried to get it, I tried to whack it. I'd miss and smash a lamp.

> *actor Johnny Depp explaining how his hotel room got smashed*

On Very Bad Excuses, Johnny Depp and, Part Two:

I can only say that I'm human and I was chasing a huge rat in the hotel room and I just kept swatting at it. I couldn't catch it, and it just jumped out the window.

> *Johnny Depp in* another *explanation of how his hotel room got smashed (reportedly he was having a fight with model/girlfriend Kate Moss who was commenting on his "shortcoming")*

On Violence, Final Word on:

I would say that anything that is indecent and violent in TV is a crime against humanity and they should shoot the head man responsible.

> *cable TV mogul Ted Turner*

On Washers of Things:

It's sinful for a woman to be in broadcasting or in some business. God made her to be a great cook, a great washer of things.
> *singer Tiny Tim*

On Watergate, Michael Jackson's Insightful Views on:

I don't know much about Watergate. It was terrible, wasn't it? I guess it was. Have you met Nixon? Is he happy? I saw him on TV last year and he looked so unhappy!
> *singer Michael Jackson in 1977, just after Watergate*

On Weddings, Romantic:

We were looking for something exciting to do, so we went to Vegas. We won some money and ended up at the Graceland Chapel, for Elvis, and that's what happened.
> *rocker Jon Bon Jovi explaining why he got married*

On Weeks, Very Long:

I've got ten pairs of trainers. That's one for every day of the week.
Samantha Fox, British pop star and model

On the Welcome Wagon, Hollywood-Style:

I know who *you* are. You don't live here, you *rent*.
actress Shannen Doherty to actress Molly Ringwald who was moving into the neighborhood to Doherty's apparent displeasure

On What It Takes to Make a Great Film, One Actor's Humble Opinion:

Me.
actor/rapper Will Smith, when asked what he thought it took to make a successful movie

On What Not to Say to a Supreme Court Justice:

Come on, Sandy baby, loosen up. You're too tight.

> *Redskins star John Riggins to his tablemate Supreme Court Justice Sandra Day O'Connor at a Washington dinner. He then proceeded to go to sleep on the floor and snore loudly during George Bush's speech.*

On What Really Matters, Donald Trump and:

You know, it really doesn't matter what [the media] write as long as you've got a young and beautiful piece of ass.

> *mogul Donald Trump*

On Why James Brolin Hates Going to Sleep:

I'll *miss* you.

> *actor James Brolin to fiancée Barbra Streisand explaining why he doesn't like going to sleep at night*

On Why We're All Here on Earth, One Celebrity's View:

We're all here for the same reason: to love me.
singer Barry Manilow to fans in Schenectady, New York

On Wisdom, Brilliant:

It's a lot better to side with a winner than a loser.
mogul Donald Trump

On Wisdom, TV Personalities and:

If you use these words [love, life, and live] in every possible combination, you'll start every day with the right attitude. Love life. Live to love. Love to live. Try it. You'll see.
television personality Robin Leach, host of Lifestyles of the Rich and Famous

On Wishes for the World:

Everyone should have enough money to get plastic surgery.
supermodel Beverly Johnson

On Wishes, Fulfilled:

If only faces could talk . . .
attributed to sports announcer Pat Summeral during the Super Bowl

On Wives, Non-PC Views about:

My notion of a wife at forty is that a man should be able to change her, like a bank note, for two twenties.
actor Warren Beatty

On Wives, Non-PC Compliments about:

Isn't she the most beautiful maid you've ever seen in your life?
actor Don Johnson on his wife Melanie Griffith, who replied, "And the most expensive, too."

On Women, One Man's View:

Most are fairly stupid. I don't like many of them.
    actor Timothy Dalton

On Women, One Man's Other View:

They're terribly hung up on how they should behave, how they ought to be, instead of just getting on with being.
    actor Timothy Dalton

On Women, Slithery:

With women, I've got a long bamboo pole with a leather loop on the end. I slip the loop around their necks so they can't get away or come too close. Like catching snakes.
    actor Marlon Brando

On Women's Golf, Enlightened Golfer's Views on:

There's nothing wrong with the ladies, God bless them; let them play. But what they're doing is eliminating much of the available time when young players can get on the course.

golfer Jack Nicklaus

On Women in Business:

I allow her to stay there because it gives her something to do.

mogul Donald Trump on why his ex-wife Ivana was still president of the Plaza hotel

On Wooden Acting:

The log is a character—or at least it has certain characteristics which can be channeled through the log lady. The log is a log—I know this log now. It has a kind of centered thing around it. It feels pretty natural. Though it's not a baby, it's a log.

actress Catherine Coulson, who played the Log Lady on TV's Twin Peaks, *explaining her costar*

On World Peace, Importance of Football and:

I can't think of a better way to spread the message of world peace than by working with the NFL and being part of Super Bowl XXVII.

> *singer Michael Jackson*

On Worldwide Universality, Observations on:

There's a certain universality of feeling which is almost worldwide.

> *actor Marlon Brando*

On the Worst Thing that Can Happen, Donald Trump's Opinion:

The worst thing a man can do is go bald. Never let yourself go bald.

> *mogul Donald Trump*

On Writing Biographies, Irritating Reasons for:

I think I really wanted to write my biography more to be able to mention that Jack Kennedy and I were friends than anything else.
comedian Jerry Lewis in Parade

On Wuggies:

I change my hairstyle every day for the show, I'm fastidious and vain about my nails and teeth and grooming and makeup, but a perfect body, forget it. Dust to dust, wuggies to wuggies.
talk show host Kathie Lee Gifford in her autobiography I Can't Believe I Said That

On Yankees, Punting:

Guest: What do you think of the Yankees?
Actress Anjelica Huston: What do I think of Yankees? I'm sorry, I don't follow football.

> *conversation at a New York party during the 1996 Yankees–Braves World Series*

On Years, Eleven-Month:

It's really great being Magic Johnson the basketball player for eight months and then just plain Earvin Johnson for the other three.

> *basketball star Magic Johnson*

On Yes-Men, Final Word on:

If there's anything I can't stand it's yes-men. When I say no, I want you to say no, too.

> *film producer Jack Warner to his publicity men*